THE EVIL WITHIN

A True Crime Series – Serial Killers

Kim Cresswell

KC Publishing

Copyright © 2020 Kim Cresswell

All rights reserved

The characters and events portrayed in this book are fictitious. Any similarity to real persons, living or dead, is coincidental and not intended by the author.

No part of this book may be reproduced, or stored in a retrieval system, or transmitted in any form or by any means, electronic, mechanical, photocopying, recording, or otherwise, without express written permission of the publisher.

ISBN 978-1-990225-00-0 1st Edition

Cover design by KC Book Cover Design

For Justin, Carla, Porter, and Peyton

In memory of Mary Beech

*Death leaves a heartache no one can heal,
love leaves a memory no one can steal.
— From a headstone in Ireland*

CONTENTS

Title Page
Copyright
Dedication
Chapter One   1
Chapter Two   24
Chapter Three   48
Chapter Four   67
Chapter Five   87
Chapter Six   123
Chapter Seven   153
Chapter Eight   173
About the Author   189
Also by Kim Cresswell   191

CHAPTER ONE

Jack Unterweger

Johann "Jack" Unterweger, the "Vienna Woods Killer" was a chameleon—one of the most clever, manipulative predators of the twentieth century and the most dangerous. Celebrity, journalist, poet, award-winning novelist, his killing spree terrorized Germany, Austria, Czechoslovakia and Los Angeles in the early 1990's. Cheered on by an endless parade of female supporters and celebrated in magazines and Austrian national radio, his 1994 trial for the murder of eleven women (three in Los Angeles and eight in Europe) was regarded as the Austrian "Trial of the Century", yet seemed to avoid major media limelight in the United States foreshadowed by the Rodney King case and the O.J. Simpson trial. After being convicted and sentenced to life in prison for nine of the eleven murders, Jack Unterweger hanged himself on June 29, 1994 in Graz, Austria.

Johann Unterweger was born August 16, 1950 in Judenburg, Styria, Austria to a Viennese waitress and prostitute, Theresia Unterweger, and an American soldier whom she later married.

"Of my paternity I knew only a name...The G.I. came from Trieste, his home was in New Jersey..."
— From *Purgatory* (Fegefeur) by Jack Unterweger

At the age of two, after his mother was convicted and jailed for fraud, the children's welfare office placed young Jack with his grandfather. Abandon by his mother at an impressionable young age, Unterweger claimed he lived in poverty with his abusive, alcoholic grandfather who had his own taste for 'ladies of pleasure'. It's not surprising the five-foot-six, boyish looking Unterweger turned to crime at an early age after spending most of his life surrounded by prostitutes and pimps. By the age of five Jack was drinking Schnapps. At nine-years-old he was chronically truant at school. During his years of "acting out" he stole cars, committed robbery and fraud then graduated to abducting a sixteen-year-old girl and tried to force her into prostitution—a chilling sign of what was yet to come.

Over the years, he was convicted over a dozen times, mainly for sexual attacks on girls in various towns and spent less than a year behind bars. The most disturbing complaint filed with the police was that of a Salzburg girl who claimed Unterweger, after offering her a ride home took her to a meadow, pushed her into the back of his car and sexually assaulted her with a steel rod while he masturbated. Shortly after the attack Unterweger was arrested and went to jail where he tried to commit suicide by swallowing a large amount of prescription pain medication he'd smuggled into his cell. Because of his suicide attempt, he was sent to a Salzburg psychiatric clinic where he stayed for a brief time, and then was released.

On June 1, 1976, a Salzburg court convicted Unterweger of the 1973 murder of Margret Schäfer, an eighteen-year-old German teenager and friend of his then girlfriend, Barbara Scholz. According to Scholz, she and Unterweger had robbed Schäfer's parent's home, and then lured Margret into a car before taking the young woman into the forest. Using the belt from her coat, Unterweger secured Margret's hands behind her back, proceeded to savagely beat her, stripped off her clothing and demanded sexual acts. When she refused, Unterweger became enraged and bludgeoned her in the head with a steel pipe. He then used her bra to strangle her before leaving her lifeless body face up in the woods and covered with leaves. The same year as the murder of Margret Schäfer, the body of twenty-five-year-old, Marica Horvath was discovered by a fisherman on the shore of Lake Salzach north of Salzburg. Clothed in only a jacket, a white sweater and naked from the waist down, her mouth was taped, her eyes swollen and black, her hands bound with a red and silver necktie.

The autopsy revealed Marica had non-violent sexual intercourse before she was savagely beaten repeatedly in the face and her legs were tied together with a pair of pantyhose. The autopsy report also disclosed Horvath was alive when she was dragged into the lake and drowned. Unterweger adamantly denied any involvement in Horveth's death, but when questioned by the police about Margret Schäfer's death, he fell apart and confessed, a move uncharacteristic of a psychopath. In court he tried to justify his actions, claiming as he beat Margret, he envisioned his mother, his anger so intense, he could not stop.

Dr. Klaus Jarosch, the forensic psychologist who examined Unterweger, declared him a sexually sadistic psychopath with narcissistic and histrionic tendencies. "He tends to sudden fits of rage and anger," Jarosch wrote. "His physical activities are enormously aggressive with sexually sadistic perversion…He is an incorrigible perpetrator."

Jack Unterweger was sentenced to life at the age of twenty-four where he would spend the next fifteen years behind bars as a model prisoner in an Austrian prison reinventing himself, manipulating and charming his way to freedom.

While incarcerated, Unterweger learned to read and write and went on to edit a prison newspaper and a literary review. He studied famous literary authors, wrote poetry, and authored numerous books, including his critically acclaimed 1984 bestselling autobiography, *Fegefeur* (Purgatory), followed by *Endstation Zuchthaus* (Terminus Prison), which won an esteemed literary prize. He even penned several children's' stories which were read on Austrian national radio. Winning over Vienna's elite, who believed that Unterweger's literature was proof he was a reformed man, Austrian publicist Guenther Nenning, headed the campaign for his release. Writers, artists, journalists and Socialist politicians crusaded for a pardon. Among them was Elfriede Jelinek, the Austrian playwright who won the 2004 Nobel Prize in Literature. Politicians and church leaders also welcomed the move. As the governor said, "We will never find a prisoner so well prepared for freedom". On May 23, 1990, Jack Unterweger was paroled.

"That life is over now," he told the press. "Let's get on with the new."

In the months following his release Unterweger became an overnight celebrity, celebrated by literary intellectuals and Vienna's chic-elite and even going as far as hosting television programs discussing criminal rehabilitation. He was featured on various other talk shows and Fegefeur (Purgatory) became a movie. With fame came money. Lots of it. He dressed in white suits, silk shirts and wore gold chains. He drove expensive fancy cars with the personal license plate, W JACK 1, and was a regular in stylish bars and nightclubs with a string of glamourous girlfriends.

He travelled extensively throughout Austria and Germany and gave readings, attended book launches, regularly appeared on television talk shows and worked as a reporter for ORF, an Austrian national public service broadcaster. But Unterweger's "new life" was a charade and it wasn't long before he returned to his old ways.

On September 15, 1990, a passerby strolling along the Vitava River in Czechoslovakia, near Prague made a horrifying discovery in the Brezany brook—the body of a woman.

Blanka Bockova was found nude. Except for a pair of gray knee-high stockings and a gold wedding ring on her finger, she was on her back covered by branches and leaves with her legs spread open. When the body was brought in for examination, it was clear she had been strangled manually with a ligature. The ligature was never found. Although there were bruises all over her body and a stab wound in one of her buttocks, there appeared to be no sign of rape. A tampon was still in place and there were no biological fluids on her or found at the scene.

Her clothing and purse were missing yet shortly after the discovery of the body, Bockova's

ID surfaced on the shore of the Vitava River, an interesting detail reminiscent of Salzberg in 1973 and the death of Marica Horvath. It appeared Bockava's killer may have also offered her a ride home but instead continued on deep into the wooded valley where she would later be murdered. Bockova was a married thirty-year-old mother who worked in a butcher shop but what she did in the evenings exposed a double life as she regularly went into the town to meet men. According to Major Hlavac of the Central Czech Police, on the night of September 14, 1990, Bockova's met her friend Martin for a drink on Wenceslause Square in Prague. When they got into an argument just before midnight, Bockova got up and left. She was last seen at approximately 11:45 pm.

Police reports would later reveal Unterweger was in Prague at the time where he claimed he was researching the city's red-light scene for a magazine article. Weeks later and five hundred kilometers away in Graz, Austria, thirty-nine-year-old Brunhilde Masser, a well-known streetwise prostitute from the red-light district went missing. She was last seen on October 26, 1990, by a taxi driver who knew her well. With prostitution legal in Austria and sexual murders rare there wasn't much concern for her disappearance until December when another prostitute vanished. Heidemarie Hammerer disappeared from her "usual" corner located close to the train station in Bregenz, the capital of Voralberg. On New Year's

Eve, almost a month after her disappearance, her body was discovered in a wooded area south of the city.

Like the murder of Blanka Bockova, Hammerer was found lying on her back partially nude covered with leaves and twigs. Her legs were bare, and a piece of cloth was stuffed in her mouth. Her body was covered with bruises and ligature marks were found on her wrists suggesting she had been tied up. She was strangled with a pair of stockings. Red and black fibres collected from her clothing would later be linked to a red scarf and a pair of black trousers found in Unterweger's closet—key evidence which would eventually be introduced at his trial.

Five miles outside of Graz, on January 5, 1991, children were playing in the woods when they made a startling find; a female body laying face down in a shallow brook partly covered with tree branches. Except for her jewelry, the body was naked, her clothing and purse missing. A wild animal appeared to have eaten part of the body in the buttock area where there were signs of a stab wound. A forensic pathologist surmised she had been strangled with a strip of cloth. Due to the advanced state of decomposition the pathologist was unable to make a decisive determination as to the cause of death. Brunhilde Masser was found approximately two months after she had vanished. On March 7, 1991, another hooker from Graz, Elfriede Schrempf, disappeared from

Volksgarten, a public park not far from where Masser disappeared. Elfriede Schrempf's skeleton was found covered with leaves in the woods south of Graz on October 5, 1991. Other than her jewellery and a pair of red socks, the remains were bare. The forensic pathologist was unable to determine the cause of death since there were no bullet wounds, knife or blunt force trauma. It was deduced she was strangled. The Gaz inspectors working on the case also concluded she was murdered by the same person who killed Brunhilde Masser.

Unaware of the murder of Blanka Bockova in Prague and with little evidence and no eyewitnesses, the Austrian police had no leads. Little did they know they were dealing with a serial killer when within a month four more prostitutes, Silvia Zagler, Sabine Moitzi, Regina Prem and Karin Eroglu vanished from the Penzing neighbourhood in Vienna. Twenty-five-year-old Sabine Moitzi's body was found on May 20, 1992 in the Vienna woods after her husband had filed a missing-person report the month before. Working as a bakery salesgirl by day, Moitzi was addicted to heroin and worked as a prostitute at night—a detail even her husband wasn't aware of. She was last seen at an intersection near the railyard of the West Train Station. Discovered naked below the waist, a leotard was yanked up around her shoulders. She was laying face down, posed in an obscene and degrading manner with her legs spread apart, her buttocks and genitals raised in the air for the entire world to see. The autopsy report would later confirm she had died from strangulation by her own stocking. The naked corpse of Karin Eroglu was found three days later by a woman searching for food for her guinea pig. Eroglu's body was laying face down under a cluster of spruce trees. Blunt-force trauma to her face indicated she had been viciously beaten. She was strangled in the same manner as Sabine Moitzi, but this time evidence was found at the scene; a ripped-off fingertip from a surgical glove which showed the kill was planned.

At the time, Regina Prem and Silvia Zagler had not been found, although it was believed their remains were somewhere deep within the Vienna woods. On June 3, ten days after the body of Karin Eroglu was discovered, a reporter for ORF strutted into the police headquarters for an interview with Chief Max Edelbacher in regard to the murders. That free-lance reporter was Jack Unterweger. He stated he was producing a story for a current affairs radio programme, *Journal Panorama*. Three days later, Unterweger's story titled, "The Fear in the Red-Light Milieu", was broadcast throughout the country, mesmerizing listeners who tuned in to hear about the secret lives of prostitutes.

The City Of Angels Meets Jack Unterweger

In 1991, Unterweger was commissioned by an Austrian magazine to write stories about crime in Los Angeles, California. When he arrived at Los Angeles International Airport on June 11th, he was dressed to the nines in white pants, snakeskin cowboy boots, and a white coat and even asked people to snap pictures of him. After renting a blue Toyota Corolla he drove downtown to the historic section of Los Angeles to the Cecil Hotel on Main Street, near Seventh, a section of the city popular with prostitutes. On the morning of June 24, Unterweger visited the LAPD Parker Center to request permission to go on a "ride-along" with officers, stating he was doing research about prostitution in the city. The following day the LAPD driving logs showed the following entry; *June 25, 1991, 11: 00 to 14: 30 hours. Austrian journalist Jack Unterweger.*

Eight days after Unterweger landed in LA, some girls were picking up litter in an empty lot surrounded by trees behind the Girl Guide center on Seventh and Frickett when they stumbled upon the body of twenty-one-year-old Shannon Exley. Exley was found on her belly, nude except for a T-shirt lifted over her breasts and was wearing blue socks. The pathologist's report revealed she was strangled with her own bra. The rest of her clothing and ID were absent from the scene. The police investigation would show on June 20, Unterweger returned the rental car with a broken windshield on the passenger side, leaving investigators to question if Exley's head hit the window as she fought for her life since there was blunt-force trauma to her skull.

A week later another female body was discovered by a homeless man in a freight company's parking lot in Boyle Heights along the LA River. The body would later be identified as thirty-three- year-old Irene Rodriguez, a married mother of four, who turned tricks to support her heroin habit. Sprawled on her back under a big rig trailer with a bra knotted around her neck, her clothes were missing, and the only other items recovered from the crime scene were a sock and the T-shirt she was wearing. A hypodermic needle was found close to her body indicating possible drug use.

On July 11, 1991, a couple of fathers, along with their children, drove to Corral Canyon Road in Malibu to watch the solar eclipse. Looking for the best vantage point above the city, they headed up an old dirt road and made a gruesome discovery yards from the road beneath a shrub; a female body laying face up. Upon closer inspection, maggots were wiggling out of the woman's nose and eyes and her T-shirt was jacked-up over her breasts. A bra was wound tightly around her neck. Identified by her fingerprints, police learned Peggy Booth, also known as Sherri Long, was a twenty-six-year-old Midwesterner with a lengthy prostitution arrest record. She was last seen on

July 3 before vanishing on Sunset Boulevard in Hollywood. As far as the pathologist could estimate from the species of maggots and their length, Booth had been dead for four to seven days. The official cause of death—asphyxia due to ligature strangulation.

Over a span of two weeks, three women were dead with a nine-day cooling off period between the murders of Shannon Exley and Irene Rodriguez and five days between the deaths of Irene Rodriquez and Peggy Booth. As speculation mounted that the women were murdered by the same perpetrator, on July 16, bras belonging to all three victims were sent for analysis. Dr. Lynne Herold with the L.A. County Sheriff's Department crime lab noted the bras were altered and the intricate knots used to make the garment into a noose were identical establishing that the women were more likely than not killed by the same person, confirming what the police already suspected. As the City of Angels and the police waited for the next murder, it never happened because Jack Unterweger had left Los Angeles and returned to Vienna.

To Catch A Killer

Back in Austria, Unterweger was interviewed on the radio several days after his return from LA, and never mentioned his trip to Los Angeles. An odd move for a man who craved the spotlight and liked to boast. Fourteen days later, on August 4, the body of Silvia Zagler, who disappeared on April 8, was discovered in the woods a few miles outside of Vienna.

With the investigation into the murders moving at a snail's pace, a break finally came when retired investigator, August Schenner, recalled a number of murders and sexual assaults he had dealt with in the 70's. The perpetrator, Jack Unterweger. The cause of death and the crime scenes from the 70's was eerily similar to the murders being committed now in the Vienna woods. He contacted Chief Max Edelbacher at police headquarters and told him they should be focusing on Jack Unterweger. When Unterweger showed up at Edelbacher's office talking about a story he was working on about the homeless in Los Angeles and Vienna, the chief told him he was one of over one hundred suspects. Unterweger blew it off as being absurd, that he couldn't possibly be a killer.

Days later, inspectors in Graz were looking into the murders of two prostitutes that happened prior to the Vienna murders, and asked if the Vienna police would assist in their investigation. Then a young prostitute came forward with an intriguing story, one about a man in a car with the license plate W JACK 1 who picked her up in Graz in the fall of 1990, days before the murders of Brunhilde Masser and Elfriede

Schrempf, and forced her to take off her clothes, tied her hands behind her back and proceeded to rape her before driving her back into town. The prostitute identified the man from a photograph as Jack Unterweger. When the Vienna DA hesitated to prosecute, Graz took over in a big way. An arrest warrant was issued but investigators soon discovered Unterweger was already on the run. Labelled a suspect and feeling the pressure, Unterweger decided it would be best for him to disappear for a while, out of the public spotlight, and the police crosshairs. He and his eighteen-year-old girlfriend, Bianca Mrak, boarded a flight to Miami. While in the sunshine state, Unterweger found his girlfriend a job as a part-time go-go dancer while he worked on his defense. He even went as far as calling the Austrian media trying to convince them of his innocence.

Through Unterweger's credit card statements investigators traced Unterweger's movements and learned he entered the United States and was in Miami, Florida. Desperate for cash, Unterweger contacted one of his old girlfriends in Vienna on February 26, claiming he was down and out and needed money. The following day the woman called him back and said her boss at the magazine she worked for was willing to pay Unterweger $10,000 dollars for an "exclusive" interview. If he agreed, he would receive a small advance which would be wired to him the next day. The balance would be paid at the interview. Unterweger was elated and jumped at the offer. Little did he know investigators were working behind the scenes and he was about to walk right into their trap. Across the street from the US Money Exchange, a team of US Marshals waited for Unterweger. When he arrived with his girlfriend, Unteweger spotted the marshals immediately. While his girlfriend went inside, he remained outside on the sidewalk. The moment Bianca emerged they walked away as if nothing was amiss, and then Unterweger took off running down an alley. He didn't get far before the US Marshals arrested him. Since Unterweger didn't fight extradition to Austria, he arrived at the Vienna airport on May 28, escorted by US Marshals. Detectives from Los Angeles flew to Vienna and questioned Unterweger about the LA prostitute murders in which he denied any involvement, saying he only was in the city to do stories on prostitutes and the homeless.

The "Trial Of The Century"

One man accused of almost a dozen murders. Austria had never seen anything like it. Being an Austrian citizen, Unterweger would be tried for the LA murders of Shannon Exley, Irene Rodriguez and Peggy Booth, and the murder of Blanka Bockova in Prague, alongside with the seven murders in Austria. Even with eleven indictments against him, Unterweger's public support didn't seem to lessen. In typical Unterweger style, he continued to give interviews boasting his innocence and how he would win. Almost two years passed before the trial began on the morning of April 20, 1994, in Graz, Austria. As the court room filled with eager spectators lucky enough to get a seat card, television crews with their flood of equipment crowded together in a special area at the front of the court room. But it wasn't long before a bomb threat forced everyone out of the room until the room was searched and the "all clear" was given. Even though Unterweger argued his own case, at times he was represented by an entertainment lawyer and a top Graz criminal defense attorney. The trial was more like question and answer period where the parties could participate because in an Austrian trial the accused is allowed to address the jury, question witnesses, and the judge and juror members are free to ask questions whenever they like.

Over the next few months, top forensic experts from around the world, specializing in DNA, microfibers, crime scene analysis, and ligature analysis, gave their testimony. Detective Jim Harper from Los Angeles, who interrogated Unterweger about the LA murders, gave his testimony as did FBI Agent Gregg McCrary, who testified about the use of VICAP (Violent Crime Analysis Program) and signature crime-scene analysis. Dr. Herold with the L.A. County Sheriff's Department crime lab testified about the knots used to construct the bras into a noose. As the prosecution presented their evidence—a psychiatric report regarding Unterweger 's criminal personality, Blanca Bockova's hair found in Unterweger's car, red fibers recovered from Brunhilde Massar's body that were consistent with the fibers from Unterweger's red scarf, support by Unterweger's followers, groupies, and the media began to swing from innocence to guilt. Some of the most compelling testimony came from retired Salzburg inspector, August Schenner. For over two decades, Schenner was determined to seek justice for the 1973 murder of twenty-five-year-old Marica Horvath found in Lake Salzach north of Salzburg. He originally tipped off the police by telling them to focus their efforts on Unterweger for the Vienna woods murders. Thankfully, they listened.

He testified about the unique necktie purchased by Unterweger in a store in Wels used to bind Horvath's hands behind her back, fashioned with the identical knot used in the sexual assault of the young prostitute in Salzburg a year earlier. He recited his jail house interview with Unterweger and how Unterweger gave a false alibi stating he was in Switzerland at the time of Horvath's murder. When the judge asked why Unterweger was never tried for the murder, Schenner explained Unterweger was already in prison for the murder of Margret Schäfer and the Salzburg D.A. felt it was useless since he could only receive one life sentence. However, it was rumored Unterweger's almighty crusaders and advocates played a large role in the decision.

The most anticipated witness to take the stand was Unterweger's ex-girlfriend, Bianca Mrak. Once his number one supporter, it was public knowledge that somewhere along the line she had a change of heart, a fact evident by her numerous interviews with the press prior to the trial.

Escorted by police into the court room, Mrak took the stand and proceeded to recite her three months with Unterweger. When the judge asked, "Was it your great love?" she stated, "For me back then, yes. When we returned from Miami, I didn't want to hurt him, and so I didn't tell the police about a couple of sacks of women's clothing I saw in his basement, as well as some panty hose in his glove compartment." With the second half of her testimony about to begin, the judge cleared the room of spectators and the press. Mrak continued on and revealed intimate details about Unterweger's sadomasochistic behaviour, the way he liked certain sexual practices, and how he tried to get her to work as a prostitute. After witness testimony concluded, Unterweger gave his final summation. "I'm counting on your acquittal, because I am not the killer. Your decision doesn't only affect me but also the murderer out there, who is laughing up his sleeve...I am innocent." Thirty days and one-hundred-sixty witnesses later, the case was finally in the jury's hands.

On June 29, 1994, at approximately 9 p.m., the jury came back with their verdict. In a vote of "six, yes" and "two, no" Unterweger was found guilty on nine of the eleven counts of murder. He was not convicted for the murders of Elfriede Schrempf and Regina Prem because their bodies were too badly decomposed for the coroner to rule on the cause of death. When the judge asked Unterweger if he had anything to say, Unterweger said, "I will appeal." Jack Unterweger was sentenced to life in prison with no chance of parole—an immense victory for the victims' families and also for August Schenner who'd made it his life mission to find justice for Marica Horvath even though Unterweger was never charged with her death.

The Final Chapter

Jack Unterweger's story would end in Graz-Karlau Prison, the third largest prison in the state of Styria. At six in the morning on June 29, Austria radio reported he had committed suicide. To escape the punishment of living the rest of his life in prison, he used a thin metal wire, a coat hook, and a cord from his track pants as a noose and hanged himself—his final act of control. Since he died before having the chance to appeal the verdict, technically under Austrian law, he is considered innocent, regardless of the guilty verdict. A technicality in the law would not bring solace to the families of the victims nor would Unterweger's suicide. Loved ones were lost forever. Women, some married, some with children who would grow up without their mothers. As for the women in Unterweger's life, like Bianca Mrak and many others, they would have to spend the rest of their lives knowing they were intimate with a serial killer.

How many serial killers are there in the United States? According to John Douglas, former Chief of the FBI's Serial Crime Unit says, "A very conservative estimate is that there are between 35-50 active serial killers in the United States" at any given time. Many serial murders go unsolved and others take decades to unravel but one thing is certain, serial killers walk among us—hiding in plain sight.

Sources

Dimond, Diane. "America's Serial Killers – How Many?" *Diane Dimond's Blog.* January 16, 2012. http://dianedimond.net.

Fegefeuer oder die Reise ins Zuchthaus (Purgatory or the Journey to Prison). Augsburg: Maro, 1983.

Leake, John. *Entering Hades: The Double Life of a Serial Killer.* Farrar, Straus and Giroux, 2007.

Leake, John. "The Vienna strangler." *The Guardian.* November 10, 2007. http://www.guardian.co.uk/.

"Austrian Charged With Killing 3 L.A. Prostitutes: Crime: Free-lance writer is indicted in Vienna in slayings of eight call girls in Europe and three here. Though there are no witnesses, police say the deaths have 'amazing similarity." *Los Angeles Times.* August 31, 1993. http://articles.latimes.com/.

Malnic, Eric. "Austrian Slayer of L.A. Prostitutes Kills Self." *Los Angeles Times.* June 30, 1994. http://articles.latimes.com/.

MacFarlane, Robert. "A Murderous Talent." January 13, 2008. http://nyti.ms/18bxwIN.

Murderpedia. "Johann "Jack" Unterweger."

http://www.murderpedia.org/.

Ramsland, Katherine. "Crime Library–Profiling, Interactive." http://www.trutv.com/.

Serial Killer Central. "Johann "Jack" Unterweger." http://www.skcentral.com.

CHAPTER TWO

The Unsolved Gilgo Beach Murders

Forty-five miles from New York City, a killer waits in the darkness on a remote stretch of highway. He parks the car. After removing his load from the trunk, he carries a bundle into the thick shoulder-high brush and dumps the burlap sack containing the dismembered body of a woman...

On December 11, 2010, a police officer and his dog were searching for a missing Jersey City prostitute when they made a gruesome discovery on the south shore of Long Island—the skeletal remains of a woman in a partially decayed burlap sack.

Unknown to police at the time, this would be the first of many grisly finds they would make along Ocean Parkway which would spawn the largest murder investigation in Long Island, New

York's history since the murders of serial killers, Joel Rifkin and Robert Schulman in the 1990's, who between them, slaughtered and dismembered more than twenty prostitutes.

By April 2011, the remains of ten people were discovered, all believed to have been killed elsewhere, all possible victims of a serial killer. Their bodies were strewn along Ocean Parkway, a desolate beach roadway surrounded by marshy grasslands, overgrown underbrush and evergreens, near the beach towns of Gilgo Beach, Oak Beach in Suffork County and Jones Beach State Park in Nassau County.

During the summer, Gilgo Beach, known to many as the "surfing capital of the east", has been a mecca for surfers since the '60s. Part of a remote barrier island south of Long Island tucked between the Atlantic Ocean and the Great South Bay. The area is an oasis for locals and tourists.

A Mystery Unfolds

On May 1, 2010, Shannan Maria Gilbert, a twenty-four-year-old Craigslist escort from Jersey City disappeared from her client, Joseph Brewer's Oak Beach home in a small gated beachfront community on Long Island after making a frantic 911 phone call at 4:51 in the morning, saying, "A man was after her."

The forty-one-year-old man from Queens who

had driven Gilbert to the home, Michael Pak, said she was "delirious" and "irrational" when she made the twenty-three-minute 911 call. She was last seen running down Anchor Way in Oak Beach after knocking on Gus Coletti's door, a neighbour of Joesph Brewer.

"She was screaming, 'Help me, help me!' and said somebody was chasing her," Gus Coletti said to police.

Two days later, police launched an extensive search for Gilbert, but she was gone. Gilbert's boyfriend at the time, Alex Diaz, 28, of Jersey City, said he last saw her on April 30.

Seven months later, on December 11, Officer John Mallia, a thirty-one year veteran with the Suffolk County Police Department and his cadaver dog were asked by the missing person's bureau to aid in the search for Gilbert in the dunes about 15 miles east of Jones Beach approximately three miles away from where she was last seen.

When Officer Mallia and his dog found the burlap sack containing the skeletal remains, the police thought they'd found Gilbert which prompted an extensive investigation. Two day later, K-9 units and police on horseback scoured over fifteen miles along the highway with the assistance of the state police, Suffolk police academy recruits, and FBI specialists. Fire truck aerial ladders stretched over the dense underbrush and pine trees as helicopters flew overhead taking aerial surveillance photographs. It wasn't long before search teams discovered three more sets of female remains near the first within 500 feet of each other, all in various states of decomposition. None belonged to Shannan Gilbert.

Investigators quickly played down the theory of a serial killer on the loose, saying they wanted to leave all options open which included surmising that the remains may possibly belong to undiscovered victims of serial killer, Joel Rifkin. Police also thought the killings might be linked to four unsolved prostitute murders in Atlantic City in 2006.

Using DNA testing and dental records, the remains were identified in as Maureen Brainard-Barnes, Melissa Barthelemy, Megan Waterman and Amber Lynn Costello. The women worked as prostitutes in the New York area and advertised their services on Craigslist and other websites, much like Gilbert. All four women were white, in their 20's, and wrapped in burlap sacks.

The First Four Victims

Maureen Brainard-Barnes

The first to disappear was Maureen Brainard-Barnes, a twenty-five-year-old mother of two from Norwich, Connecticut who juggled a trio of jobs; cashier, telemarketer and Craigslist escort. On July 6, 2007, she left for New York for the weekend to meet a client at a Time Square motel and never returned home on Monday as planned. After a search by family members of the 42nd street area turned up nothing they filed a missing person report with the New York Police Department.

A break in the case came approximately three weeks later when investigators learned Brainard-Barnes' cell phone was turned on in the vicinity of Fire Island off Long Island. Reportedly, a "connection was made" but no further details were released to the public. She was last seen on July 9, in Manhattan.

According to a posting on the Internet, "Maureen was a mother who loved her kids dearly. Maureen was a poet who wrote the most amazing poems. Maureen was a sister who was always there for them. Maureen was a person. A beautiful woman inside and out." Maureen Brainard-Barnes' children were eight and one when she vanished.

Melissa Barthelemy

Melissa Barthelemy was last seen on July 12, 2009, sitting outside her Bronx apartment building on Underhill Avenue. To her family, she was a "sweet, outgoing girl who grew up in Buffalo, graduated from South Park High, and attended cosmetology school".

Barthelemy was a twenty-four-year-old hairstylist and escort who advertised her services on Craigslist and occasionally worked for James Bond Entertainment, an escort agency. On the afternoon, the petite blonde disappeared, a security camera at her bank caught her depositing $1000.00 into her bank account, money she reportedly earned from a date the night before. Barthelemy charged anywhere from $100 for 15 minutes to $1000 overnight and advertised 'outcalls', agreeing to only go to the client's place.

The following day Barthelemy stopped answering her phone and text messages. Worried family members filed a missing person's report, but New York City Police wouldn't act immediately. It would be ten days before they began their investigation by canvassing the neighbourhood, extracting DNA from her toothbrush and examining her phone records. Her phone records revealed someone accessed her voicemail on the night she disappeared, and the calls were traced to a cell tower in Massapequa, Long Island. Investigators visited two motels, the Budget Inn and Best Western, spoke to staff, and reviewed the security tapes. They came up empty.

A week after Barthelemy went missing, her younger sister received seven taunting calls on Melissa's cellphone over a period of five weeks. *The New York Daily News* reported, the man on the phone, who may be Barthelemy's killer, asked Amanda if she knew her sister's profession, and described Melissa as "a whore." The last call was made in August 2009 when the caller stated he had killed Barthelemy.

The police traced a few of the calls to midtown Manhattan and to Massapequa, however, the calls ended before investigators were able to pinpoint the caller's location.

Megan Amelia Waterman

Twenty-two-year-old, Megan Waterman was described as "moon-faced and bubbly".

A single mother of a young daughter and an escort from Scarborough, Maine, Waterman disappeared in May after travelling to New York on Memorial Day weekend with her boyfriend at the time, twenty-one-year-old, Akeem Cruz, the man responsible for getting Waterman interested in using online sites like Craigslist to sell herself. He was more than her boyfriend; he was her pimp. In October 2009, she was arrested in a hotel in Bethpage, Long Island for prostitution after agreeing to carry out sexual acts for money with an undercover officer. During the same year, on two separate occasions, she was arrested for theft and for the use and sale of drug paraphernalia.

Waterman was last seen at a Holiday Inn Express in Hauppauge, N.Y., on June 6. When the police searched her hotel room, they found her clothing, makeup, and her cellphone. Surveillance footage showed Waterman left the hotel around 1:30 a.m., alone and on foot.

When police questioned her boyfriend, Cruz told investigators Megan checked into the hotel alone. He last saw her around 8 p.m. on June 5 and talked to her by cellphone at 1:30 a.m. on the morning of June 6. Although, Cruz was cleared as a suspect in Waterman's disappearance, on April 2012, in a federal court in Brooklyn, he plead guilty to transporting Waterman and other women across state lines from Maine to New York for prostitution. He was sentenced to 3 years in prison on January 4, 2013.

Amber Lynn Costello

The night Amber Costello disappeared she had booked a "date" with a stranger after negotiating with him on the phone; the agreed-upon price of $1500, a fee much higher than her usual rate. She headed out for her date and never returned. Costello was last seen in North Babylon, Long Island, on September 2, 2010. Sadly, a missing person's report was never filed.

Costello was raised near Wilmington, N.C., and moved to Cleardale, Florida. According to a close friend, Costello was "a kind, loving, beautiful person". Working in the sex trade since the age of seventeen, she developed a heroin addiction early on, a demon she would battle throughout her short life. By twenty-seven she had been married and divorced twice. During the last year of her life, Kimberly Overstreet, Costello's older sister, brought her to New York and got her into a rehab. She also found faith. Described as a "natural at helping people through dark times and using her own experiences to comfort others", Rev. Wayne Griffiths, senior pastor of First Baptist Church of Babylon said, "She had empathy. She used these characteristics to help others."

Once sober, Amber Costello moved into an apartment, but the lure of prostitution yanked her back into drugs, and it wasn't long before she was selling her body to feed her addiction. She died seven days before her twenty-eighth birthday.

While the investigation moved forward, Suffolk County District Attorney Thomas Spota said during a news conference that "each of the four had been killed elsewhere and dumped on the beach. I believe it is, yes [a serial killer]. I think it fits within the definition of what a serial killer would be." He also said the causes of death appeared to be "substantially similar" but did not go into any further details at the time.

Criminologist Casey Jordan told *CBS News' "The Early Show"* the killer or killers may have a sexual motivation. Jordan said the police are likely dealing with a "power control killer or hedonistic lust killer" since the women were lured through Craigslist.

"What activities these victims may have engaged in prior to their murders does not matter," Suffolk County Police Commissioner Richard Dormer said. "They were young women whose lives were cut tragically short."

As rumors swirled the killer might be a Suffolk or Nassau County resident, possibly a neighbor living near Gilgo or someone who commuted regularly through the area, police said they didn't expect to find any more victims and would search the area again when the weather turned milder.

When winter finally loosened its icy grip on New York and warmer weather arrived, a surprise awaited police—more bodies.

On March 29, 2011, an officer was scanning the dunes from the highway, "when he noticed an item that caught his attention," Suffolk County Police Commissioner Richard Dormer said.

Upon closer inspection, it was the head, hands and forearm of a woman. Two days later, three more sets of remains were unearthed by investigators a mile east from the first four but there were differences between the latest discoveries and the first four. These remains weren't in burlap sacks and they had been on the beach much longer than the original four victims signalling the possibility of a second killer or a copycat killer.

Again, none of the remains belonged to Shannan Gilbert who went missing May 1, 2010. However, the latest discoveries prompted authorities to revisit the Oak Beach area where Gilbert was last seen alive.

Jessica Taylor

The fifth victim was identified on May 9, 2011 as twenty-year-old Jessica Taylor, a prostitute who worked in Washington D. C., and Manhattan before she vanished in 2003. Taylor may never have been identified if it hadn't been for a Washington police officer scanning police bulletins of unidentified remains when he noticed a tattoo of wings and the words "Remy's Angel" on the back of the torso found in 2003 in Manorville fit her description. The tattoo had been mutilated and cut by the killer in hopes of making identification more difficult.

Her nude torso had been discovered in Manorville near the Long Island Expressway, about 40 miles to the east. With a connection now established, police realized they were dealing with two dumping grounds.

Taylor grew up in upstate New York and was estranged from her family. In February 2003, she was arrested numerous times in New York City on a variety of charges including; soliciting an undercover officer, possession of stolen property and assaulting a police aide. She plead guilty and was sent to Riker's Island jail on Feb. 25, 2003. She was released on April 28, 2003. Taylor was last seen on July 26, 2003 prostituting near the Port Authority Bus Terminal in Manhattan.

In hopes of identifying more victims, Suffolk County officials released sketches on September 20, 2011 of an unidentified male and female.

Jane Doe 6's hands, skull, and right foot were found on April 4. DNA extracted from the remains was linked to a torso found in Manorville, N.Y., in November 2000. Jane Doe 6 was described as being between the ages of 18 and 35 and approximately five-foot-two.

"To narrow the focus this woman would have been last seen alive in the late summer or fall in 2000…may have had a tattoo or other identifiable characteristic on her right ankle," Police Commissioner Richard Dormer said.

The second sketch was of an Asian male found dressed in women's clothing rendering speculation he was a cross-dressing prostitute. The man died of blunt-force trauma and was believed to be between 17 and 23 years old and approximately 5-foot-6. He was missing his top and bottom molars as well as a front tooth, police said. He had been dead for five to ten years.

Also released were photographs of jewelry found near two other victims believed to be a mother and her toddler. Investigators had made a DNA match between the pair.

"It is likely that these two individuals were mother and child," Suffolk County Police Commissioner Richard Dormer said.

According to police, the toddler was described as a "non-Caucasian" and was wearing hoop earrings and a necklace. She was believed to be between 16 and 32 months old. The child's mother was wearing two bracelets; one bracelet with X's and O's containing stones resembling diamonds and a gold snake chain.

"We are hopeful that the release of this additional information will aid our investigation in helping identify the unknown victims and their killer or killers," Dormer said at the press conference.

Authorities also stated that a forensic artist was working on a third sketch of a woman whose legs were found in April. DNA from her remains was linked to remains discovered in a garbage bag in Davis Park on Fire Island in Nassau County, N.Y., in 1996.

Police sources told ABC *News* that all of the victims appeared to have been killed elsewhere, dismembered, and then transported to the beach areas and dumped. Bodies that have been dumped are difficult cases to solve because there are no neighbours to question, no video surveillance to watch and witnesses are usually non-existent.

In November 2011, Suffolk County Police Commissioner Richard Dormer said that detectives believe one person is responsible for the murders on Gilgo Beach. "We've had the same dumping ground, sex workers, young women—even though there were the Asian male and the toddler—but we think they were connected to the sex trade in some way. And these common denominators indicate we have the one person committing these crimes."

Authorities previously thought as many as three killers were responsible.

Shannan Gilbert

Shannan Gilbert's family would finally have her home nineteen months after she vanished. In a remote area of Gilgo Beach, Suffolk County Police brought in bulldozers to remove brush in a marshy area and spent the early morning searching with K-9 and marine units as well as with metal detectors and amphibious vehicles. They discovered Gilbert's pocketbook, jeans, cellphone, lip gloss, and shoes on December 12, 2011 close to the Oak Beach neighbourhood where she was last seen alive. The following morning, detectives found Shannan Gilbert's remains in a different area.

Even though the medical examiner was unable to determine the cause of death from what was left of Gilbert, only hair and bones, and despite similarities to the other cases, police believe she accidentally drowned in the marsh as she tried to make her way to the road.

Suffolk County Police Commissioner Richard Dormer said. "We surmise that's what happened to Shannan."

But Gilbert was found on the other side of the marsh where she would have had to travel a quarter mile by foot from where she was last seen, walk through dense bush in waist-high water and quicksand like areas. Why would she unbuckle her sandals and take off her tight-fitting jeans before going through the marsh if she was running for her life? It doesn't make sense. And how could she have drowned in ankle-deep water?

Her family believes she was murdered.

The case has gained worldwide attention including an A&E television special, a special edition of "48 Hours Mystery" titled "Long Island Serial Killer" which aired on July 12, 2011, the investigation has also drawn a lot of criticism from family members who have accused the police of incompetency and not keeping them updated on the investigation. A lawsuit was filed on November 15, 2011, by Mari Gilbert (Shannan's mother) against the Suffolk County Police Department in the hopes of getting answers as to what happened to Gilbert the night she disappeared.

Other Possible Victims

On May 22, 2011, one hundred miles east of Gilgo Beach, a decomposed, headless body washed ashore on Amagansett Beach. An autopsy revealed the remains belonged to a slightly built young male, 20 to 30 years old, and it appeared the body had been in the water for months. There were no obvious signs of trauma, gunshot wounds or breaks to the bones. The left leg from the knee down was missing due to decomposition. A finger had also been missing, Chief Ed Ecker said, but was found during the police dive team's search of Gardiner's Bay, near where the body was found. Police divers were not able to locate the skull.

In May 2011, Long Island police revisited two other similar unsolved murders of prostitutes. Tanya Rush, 39, a mother of three from Brooklyn. Her dismembered body was found in a small suitcase in June 2008 on the shoulder of the

Southern State Parkway in Bellmore, New York. On a memorial posting on the Internet, the daughter of Tanya Rush said, "I received a call saying that my mother had been killed. Her body was fully dismembered and parts of her are still missing. She had been separated and placed in plastic bags and stored inside of a suitcase. There have been no arrests or suspects in her case."

Police have not released the identity or revealed any information regarding the second case.

On February 18, 2012, skeletal human remains were discovered by a man walking his 13-year-old German short-haired pointer in Manorville, near Wading River Rd. The remains were found bundled in a bed sheet and wrapped in a plastic bag with duct tape in the densely wooded area about 300 feet north of the road.

"I thought it was a rock at first, but it was kind of weird," Matt Samuel said. "Then I looked a little closer and saw where the plates fuse together so I knew it was a skull. It didn't look like any animal skull I'd ever seen."

Police said they believe the remains have likely been in the woods for about five years and they have not linked this case to the other murders claiming it was too early to tell. The remains were found in the same Manorville area as Jane Doe 6's torso in 2000 and Jessica Taylor torso in 2003. A possible coincidence?

A skeleton was discovered on January 23, 2013 by a woman walking her dog along the shore at the end of Sheep Lane in Lattingtown, Long Island, near Oyster Bay. The remains are believed to belong to a woman between the ages of twenty and thirty years old, possibly Asian. She was wearing a gold pig pendant which may be a reference in Asian culture to "The Year of the Pig". Investigators believe she may have been buried prior to Hurricane Sandy in October 2012.

"The best lead we have so far is the necklace," Detective Lt. John Azzata of the Nassau County Police homicide squad said.

Since the discovery of the first set of remains in December 2010, there have been many theories and opinions such as; the Long Island serial killer is a seasonal worker, maybe a fisherman from the nearby town or perhaps a drifter. Others believe the killer could be a police officer or a local living in one of the beach communities.

"The person has got to be comfortable with the locations," Police Commission Dormer said, citing the long distances between Manorville and Gilgo Beach, and from Davis Park to Gilgo Beach. "That's the theory, that it's a Long Islander. That's a huge distance, so somebody has to be familiar with the Long Island area and comfortable with that area." Dormer also said the case remains a "high priority," and police are still "actively investigating."

"I believe that there is one killer that is haunting Long Island, and I believe there is a really good chance he is a seasonal visitor," said Dr.

Scott A. Bonn, a serial killer expert and assistant professor of sociology at Drew University. "[The killer] is intimately familiar with the area and comfortable with it. I think there is a very good chance that he grew up in the area," Bonn added.

In late 2012, Lucius Crawford, a sixty-year-old ex-con was named in the murders but Suffolk Police Department later released a statement saying, "At this point in time there does not appear to be any reason to suspect that Crawford has any involvement with the homicides that have occurred in the last several years where the bodies were discovered in the vicinity of Gilgo Beach."

Suffolk County Police Commissioner, Richard Dormer said the case remains "high priority," and that police are "still actively investigating."

As of November 2013, no arrests have been made into the Giglo Beach murders and police have not released names of any possible suspects in the case.

It was because of Shannan Gilbert's disappearance, her message from the grave that triggered a search which uncovered a serial killer's deadly rampage. How many more victims have yet to be discovered? Has the killer moved to another dumping ground? What secrets, if any, were washed into the ocean after Superstorm Sandy hammered the New York coastline in October 2012?

"This guy [the killer] is meticulous, sadistic and smart. I suspect he's probably a professional

—extremely charming and disarming," Dr. Scott Bonn said. "He's not going to stop, and the nature of the victims' lifestyle (the fact that prostitutes often go unreported when they are missing) makes them the ideal prey. For all we know, he may have another dumping ground already."

Sources

The Associated Press, "Long Island deals with latest notorious murder case, spurred by missing Jersey City prostitute." *NJ.com*. December 10, 2011. http://www.nj.com/.

Buffa, Denise. "Sister of Victim Won't Stop Tracking Case Until Serial Killer Is Caught." *The Courant*. March 25, 2012. http://articles.courant.com/.

Chang, Sophia, Chau Lam, Nicholas Spangler. "Faces of the Gilgo Beach victims." *Long Island Newsday.* April 24, 2011. http://www.newsday.com/.

CNN Wire Staff. "Police: Remains are believed to be those of Shannan Gilbert." *69 FMZ-TV.* December 13, 2011. http://www.wfmz.com/

Daily Mail Reporter. "'Craigslist Ripper' police reveal up to FOUR killers may have dumped bodies on Long Island beach as new victim is identified." *Daily Mail*. May 11, 2011. http://www.dailymail.co.uk/.

Dooley, C. Emily. "Gilgo victim a natural helper." *Long Island Newsday*. February 5, 2011. http://www.newsday.com

Eeposito, Richard, Josh Einiger, Jessica Hopper.

"Long Island Serial Killer Hunt: Police Release Sketches of Victims." *Psyhcowatcher.* October 21, 2011. http://psychowatcher.wordpress.com/.

Eltman, Frank. "Police: Maine woman 1 of 4 dead near NY beach." *The Huffington Post.* January 19, 2011. http://www.huffingtonpost.com/.

Gallucici, Jaclyn. "Shannan Gilbert's Disappearance: Three Years Later." *Long Island Press.* May 1, 2013. http://www.longislandpress.com/.

Gardiner, Sean, Eileen Markey. "Drawn to City's Glamour, Cut Down by a Serial Killer." *The Wall Street Journal.* January 24, 2011. http://on.wsj.com/1aIZOXm.

Hawkins, Kristal. "The Long Island Ripper". *Crime Library.* http://www.trutv.com/.

Helfand, Lorri. "Police say former Pinellas woman, found dead in New York, could be victim of a serial killer." *Tampa Bay Times.* January 27, 2011. http://www.tampabay.com/.

Hench, David. "Man pleads guilty to prostitution-related charge in Waterman case." *Portland Press Herald.* April 12, 2012. http://www.pressherald.com/.

Hutchinson, Bill, Joe Stephanky. "Gold pig necklace key to revealing ID of remains found in Lattingtown, though serial killer connection undetermined." *NY Daily News.* January 23, 2013.

http://www.nydailynews.com/.

Kolker, Robert. "First Lost, Then Murdered." *Slate*. July 9, 2013. http://www.slate.com/.

Lohr, David. "Long Island Serial Killer Is Seasonal Visitor, Expert Scott Bonn Contends." *Huffington Post Canada*. February 21, 2012. http://www.huffingtonpost.com/.

Martinez, Edecio. "Long Island Serial Killer? A "hedonistic lust killer," says profiler." *CBS News*. April 5, 2011. http://www.cbsnews.com/.

McLaughlin, Michael. "Long Island Serial Killer Case: Suffolk County District Attorney Blasts Rumors." *Huffington Post Canada*. May 9, 2012. http://www.huffingtonpost.com/.

Ottone, Robert. *"The Gilgo Beach Murders: Two Years Later."* Longisland.com. December 9, 2012. http://www.longisland.com/.

NBC News and msnbc.com staff. "Police push to find woman whose case led them to Long Island bodies." *NBC News*. December 1, 2011. http://nbcnews.to/1btxLfQ.

Parascandola, Rocco, Barry Paddock, Lukas I. Alpert. "Phone of slain craigslist hooker used in Times Square, MSG to taunt victim's sister, sources say." *NY Daily News*. January 26, 2011. http://www.nydailynews.com/.

Pelisek, Christine. "Terror on Long Island." *The Daily Beast.* April 17, 2011. http://www.thedailybeast.com/.

Pelisek, Christine. "The Serial Killer Victim's Secret Life." *The Daily Beast.* April 24, 2011. http://www.thedailybeast.com/.

Pelisek, Christine. "Shannan Gilbert Body Likely Found, New York Police Say." *The Daily Beast.* December 13, 2011. http://www.thedailybeast.com/

Ramos, Andrew. "Sketches Of Victims, Photos Released In Gilgo Beach Investigation." *Chicago Tribune.* September 20, 2011. http://www.chicagotribune.com/.

Riley, John. "Gilgo victim Megan Waterman's pimp sentenced to prison." *Long Island Newsday.* January 4, 2013. http://www.newsday.com/.

Schupp-Miller, Kimberly. "Another Craigslist killer? Bodies of 4 women ID'ed." *Wis TV.* January 25, 2013. http://bit.ly/h8X3Ss.

Smith, Graham. "Missing prostitute feared to be one of four victims 'Craigslist Killer' dumped on a New York beach." *The Daily Mail.* December 16, 2010. http://www.dailymail.co.uk/.

Van Sant, Will. "Chilling find links LI dumping grounds." *Long Island Newsday.* May 9, 2011.

http://www.newsday.com/.

Vecsey K, Taylor (Editor). "Autopsy: Headless Body Wasn't Decapitated." *EastHamptonPatch*. May 25, 2011. http://easthampton.patch.com/.

Wikipedia. "Long Island serial killer." http://en.wikipedia.org/

WNBC. "Police believe single serial killer behind Long Island bodies." *NBC News*. November 30, 2011. http://nbcnews.to/1dAWxxp.

"In Memory of Tanya Rush." *Causes.* October 31, 2009. http://www.causes.com/.

"Long Island Serial Killer: That Other Crime Scene." *The Surveillance Report.* October 10, 2012 http://cctvservicesblog.com/.

"Police Investigating Skeletal Remains Found In Manorville." *CBS New York.* February 18, 2012. http://newyork.cbslocal.com/2012/02/18/.

"Police: Pocketbook, Personal Items Found Believed To Be Shannan Gilbert's." *CBS New York.*
December 7, 2011. http://newyork.cbslocal.com/2011/12/07

CHAPTER THREE

Joseph Franklin: Race War

Joseph Paul Franklin was born James Clayton Vaughan Jr., in Mobile, Alabama on April 13, 1950. As the second of four children he was the son of an alcoholic butcher, James Clayton Vaughn Sr. and a waitress, Helen Rau. Growing up in immense poverty in an all-white public housing project, he was abused regularly by his parents especially his mother who would wake him and his brother in the middle of the night and beat them. According to Franklin's sister, Carolyn, their parents would scream, swear and beat them relentlessly. In an interview in 2013 with Kyung Lah, *CNN*, Franklin stated that while growing up "he was fed such a poor diet that it affected his development. I've always been least 10 years or more behind other people in their maturity."

Franklin was a gun lover like most children and teenagers and would go on to become a skillful marksman but something darker lurker also inside him at an early age. He became an animal abuser finding great enjoyment in mistreating creatures he discovered in his yard.

At the age of 17, he left his schooling behind at Murphy High School and began getting into regular altercations with the police. Unable to join the draft after losing almost of the all the vision in his right eye in a childhood accident which left him legally blind, he was arrested for assault, disorderly conduct and carrying a concealed on numerous occasions.

Shortly afterwards, he became preoccupied with Evangelical Christianity and churches in general by visiting every church in Mobile. But his religious beliefs changed drastically after reading a copy of Adolf Hitler's political manifesto, *Mein Kamf.* It was the beginning of his hate-filled mission which God had told him that he wanted him to begin a race war.

He would practice Nazi salutes in a mirror and wore a swastika on to his shirt. He also fantasied that he was a member of the Hell's Angels complete with ripped jeans and a knife in his pocket, minus the motorcycle.

Sometime around Valentine's Day 1968, he met a neighbourhood girl, 16-year-old Bobbie Louise Dorman and two weeks later they were married. But the marriage didn't last long after he had beat his new bride numerous times to the point, she was terrified he would kill her. They were divorced after four months.

After Franklin left his wife, he also left the Nazi movement and he made his home in Atlanta where he joined the fascist National States Rights Party and began selling the racist newspaper, *The Thunderbolt*. Later on, he became a member of the National Socialist White People's Party and joined the Ku Klux Klan in 1976 but quit after a few months because he wasn't happy with the Klan's lack of violence.

That same year he sent a threatening letter to newly elected President Jimmy Carter, threatening to kill him for his pro-civil rights views. He also planned to shoot Jesse Jackson, but Jackson's security men made it impossible for him to carry out his agenda.

He continued to spend most of his life as a drifter, traveling along the east coast searching for opportunities to rid the world of those who he believed where inferior and enemies to the white race, mainly African American and Jews.

Four years following the death of his mother Franklin decided at the age of 26 to change his name to Joseph Paul Franklin in honor of Nazi propaganda minister Paul Joseph Goebbels and Benjamin Franklin. He even tried to connect himself to serial killer Charles Manson by having the words 'Helter Skelter' tattooed on his arm.

On Labor Day he tailed a vehicle carrying an African-American man and his white companion for almost 10 miles to a dead end where they stop and then sprayed the interracial couple with Mace. This would be his first known racially motivated attack and soon his attacks would escalate into murder. In 1977 Franklin joined Alabama National Guard and robbed a bank in Atlanta. As his racism and fixation with anti-Jewish literature grew, his next opportunity was planned with meticulous care in Washington DC, on July 25, 1977, in the early morning under a blanket of darkness while the world slept.

At 3:17 a.m., outside of the home of Jewish pro-Isreal lobbyist, Morris Amitay and his family, Franklin detonated a trunk load of dynamite. Although the home was severely damaged Amitay and his family escaped uninjured. But Franklin didn't stop there.

On July 29, 1977, the Beth Sholom synagogue in Chattanooga, Tennessee was bombed. Luckily the bomb went off an hour after services were done. No one was injured to Franklin's dismay. After the incident, he realized he had set the bomb off at the wrong time, an hour later than he should have.

Following his failed attempt to kill as many Jews as possible he drove to Columbus, Ohio and robbed a bank on August 2, 1977. Afterwards, he traveled to Madison, Wisconsin and robbed another bank on August 7.

After robbing another bank in Little Rock, Arkansas, Franklin next drove to Dallas, Texas where he purchased a 30-06 rifle with a telescopic sight. From there he made his way to St. Louis, Missouri and scoured the city for his next opportunity; the Brith Shalom Kneseth Israel Congregation in Richmond Heights. He would later go on to say he used the yellow pages of a phone book to select his target where he could slaughter Jews.

Armed with ten-inch nails, a guitar case and a bicycle for his getaway, he hammered the nails into a telephone pole which he would later use as a rifle rest. After removing the serial number from the weapon, he wiped down the gun, ammunition and the guitar case of any possible fingerprints and then placed the gun inside the case and hid in it the bushes close to the synagogue.

On October 7, 1977, just before 1:00 p.m. while worshipers left the synagogue after a bar mitzvah and headed to their vehicles, Franklin hid in the shadows of the tall grass yards away behind a telephone pole with his high-powered rifle aimed and ready.

The first bullet tore into 42-year-old Gerald Gordon's left side of his chest. He later died at the old St. Louis County Hospital in front of his wife and three children from the loss of blood following the extensive damage to many of his internal organs. Another bullet grazed Steven Goldman's shoulder and William Ash was wounded in the hip and the left hand resulting in the loss of his baby finger.

When he was done emptying the rifle Franklin quickly abandoned the weapon and guitar case then pedalled his bicycle to a parking lot close by where his car was parked then left St. Louis. His killing spree would continue for another three years.

❖ ❖ ❖

During 1978, Franklin robbed three more banks. One in Louisville, Kentucky, Atlanta, Georgia and one in Montgomery, Alabama. In February he killed Johnny Brookshire, 22, and paralyzed his white girlfriend, Joy Williams, 23, in Atlanta, Georgia.

On March 6, 1978, in Lawrenceville, Georgia, he purchased a .44 caliber rifle and ambushed Hustler publisher, Larry Flynt, who was facing obscenity charges. As Flynt left the courthouse two shots hit him leaving him barely alive and paralyzed from the waist down. He also seriously wounded Gene Reeves, Flynt's lawyer as the bullet tore through his arm then into numerous internal organs. He later recovered from his injuries.

Days before the shooting as his anger grew Franklin checked into a motel and truly believed that if he shot Flynt that he would easily shut down the magazine for good. Unknown at the time, Franklin had been stalking Fynt

During a prison interview in 2013, 63-year-old Franklin explained to Kyung Lah, CNN, why he decided to shoot Flynt.

> *"I saw that interracial couple he had, photographed there, having sex,' he says. Franklin is referring to the December 1975 issue of Hustler that featured several photos of a black man with a white woman. 'It just made me sick. I think whites marry with whites, blacks with blacks, Indians with Indians. Orientals with orientals. I threw the magazine down and thought, I'm gonna kill that guy."*

Four months later on July 29, 1978, Franklin traveled to Chattanooga. Hiding next to a Pizza Hut he killed Bryant Tatum, an African American using a 12-gauge shotgun and shot Tatum's white girlfriend, Nancy Hilton, who survived the ordeal.

Late in 1978, Franklin returned to Alabama and married 16-year-old Anita Carden, a teenager he'd met in an ice-cream parlor at the DeKalb County Courthouse. Together they had a daughter, but it soon came apparent that his newfound fatherhood wasn't as strong a bond as his white-supremacy obsession. Seven months passed and the father-to-be was long gone leaving only a few food items in the cupboards for his wife.

On January 12, 1980, Franklin shot and killed a mentally retarded African American named Lawrence E. Reese, 23, while working at a Church's

Fried Chicken Restaurant in Indianapolis as well as 19-year-old Leo Thomas Watkins six days later on January 14.

As the summer heat bared down on the residents of Georgia, Harold McIver, a 27-year-old African American and manager of a Taco Bell who had contact with white women was fatally shot through a window in Doraville on July 12, 1979. Franklin would later confess but was never tried for the crime.

In early May of 1980, he killed Raymond Taylor at Burger King in Falls Church, Virginia. Later that month Franklin shot and severely wounded civil rights activist and Urban League president Vernon Jordan, Jr. outside of the Marriott Inn in Fort Wayne, Indiana after witnessing him with a white woman.

Less than two weeks passed and on June 8 at 11:30 p.m, Darrell Lane, 14, and Dante Evans Brown, two African American cousins, were heading to a twenty-four-hour convenience store in the Bond Hill area of Cincinnati. Unknown to them Franklin was waiting on a railroad trestle with a .44 caliber rifle determined to shoot an interracial mixed couple. When he didn't spot exactly what he was looking for he decided to shoot and kill the boys instead.

Seven days later in Johnstown, Pennsylvania, Franklin concealed himself on a densely wooded slope 100 yards away and watched a 22-year-old African American, Arthur Dale Smothers, and his white 16-year-old girlfriend, Kathereen Mikula, walk across a downtown bridge. Both were killed by two shotgun blasts.

In June following the killings, Franklin drove to Burlington, North Carolina and robbed yet another bank.

Nancy Santomero, 19, and Vicki Durian, 26, were hitchhiking in Pocahontas County, West Virginia on June 25, 1980. According to an Ohio assistant prosecutor, Franklin claimed that he'd picked up the two white girls and decided to kill them using a .44 Ruger pistol because one of the girls had mentioned she had an African American boyfriend. Jacob Beard of Florida was originally convicted and imprisoned for the murders in 1993. He was freed in 1999 for a crime he did not commit.

On August 20, 1980, Franklin's racially driven multi-state crime and murder spree continued. Near Liberty Park in Salt Lake City, he killed two African American men, 18-year-old Ted Fields, and his 20-year-old friend, David Martin, an Eagle Scout after they were jogging with two white female 15-year-old friends. The men had barely made it across a well-lit intersection at 500 East at 900 South when they were hit at approximately 10:15 p.m. Franklin was tried on federal civil rights charges and charged with first-degree murder in both the killings.

Franklin also killed two African American children in Cincinnati, three female hitchhikers, as well as a white 15-year-old prostitute, Mercedes Lynn Masters, because the girl had sex with African American men.

In September 1980, Florence Kentucky police caught up with Franklin by accident. When they ran a record check an outstanding warrant popped up. He was arrested on suspected car theft charges. A search of his vehicle led to evidence that suggested multiple associations to the racially motivated sniper attacks.

As the authorities began to reconstruct the string of hate-crime murders and attacks that spanned from the South to the Midwest, they discovered Franklin had used more than 17 different aliases to stay under the authorities radar, changed his weapons and cars on regular basis and even changed his looks by coloring his hair to the point it began falling.

Five hours following his arrest he found a way to escape the building through a window and fled, triggering a nationwide manhunt. Without a car or his guns, he wouldn't get far, his freedom short-lived especially with the FBI on his trail.

A few weeks later while giving blood in Florida at a skid row blood bank, a nurse recognized Franklin's tattoos from police descriptions of a suspect being sought for numerous murders and immediately called the authorities. FBI agents arrested 30-year-old Franklin at Sera-Tec Biologicals in Lakeland on October 28, 1980.

At first, he denied that he was the killer that the police were looking for. He'd even gone as far as to try unsuccessfully to scrape off the American eagle tattoo on his left arm and the Grim Reaper tattoo on his right. But he made a crucial mistake by signing in at his last known address as James C. Vaughan Jr., at the $2.50 a night flophouse in Tampa, Florida giving away his identity.

The FBI believed Franklin had robbed so many banks to finance is a racial-driven objection. It was also discovered that he collected manuals on police procedures which were found in the trunk of his brown Camaro making it easier for him to dodge the authorities.

On November 7, he was extradited to Salt Lake City, Utah and arraigned on the charges involving Ted Fields and David Martin. He was convicted on March 4, 1981, of violating the civil rights of Fields and Martin and was sentenced to two consecutive life sentences. During sentencing, Franklin called prosecutor Steven Snarr "a liar" and "little faggot" and thrust himself at African-American civil rights attorney with the U.S. Department of Justice, Richard Roberts, and called him a trained ape then went after the judge but was immediately shackled before he could make it a few feet.

During the state trial in June regarding the two murder charges for killing Fields and Martin, Flanklin was convicted and received two more life sentences. He was briefly sent to the Medial Center for Federal Prisoners in Springfield, *Michigan.* By the end of January 1982, he was transferred to the United States Penitentiary in Marion, Illinois to begin serving his life sentences.

While incarcerated, the proclaimed racist was stabbed 15 times in the neck and abdomen by a group of African Americans three days after he arrived at the prison and was wheelchair bound due to his wounds. He remained in solitary confinement for his own protection for almost three decades.

In 1983 Franklin confessed to the shooting of Larry Flynt as well as for the bombing of Morris Amitay's house in Washington DC. The following year he admitted to the murder of Rebecca Bergstrom, the murders of Santomero and Durian, the Chattanooga synagogue bombing and shooting Aplhonse Manning and Toni Schween.

He is sentenced to 15-20 years for the bombing and 6-10 years for possession of explosives. Seven months later in February 1986, Franklin is convicted in Wisconsin for killing Manning and Schwenn and received two consecutive life sentences.

As he continued to confess his crimes one after another, on February 27, 1997, he was found guilty for the cold-blooded sniper killing of Gerald Gordon. During his 1997 trial, Franklin represented himself and requested that the jury sentence him to death then went on to tell the court that his only attrition was that killing Jews wasn't legal.

It took the jury less than 40 minutes to convict him and Franklin was sentenced to death by lethal injection.

Larry Flynt, a strong opponent of the death penalty, chose to put aside his own pain at the hands of Franklin and spoke against Franklin's execution, stating that capital punishment was about vengeance and at all about justice. Flynt even went as far with the assistance of the American Civil Liberties Union and went to court determined to stop the execution.

According to the Hollywood Reporter, in an article penned by Larry Flynt in October 2013, he said would have loved a little alone time with Franklin along "with a pair of wire cutters and pliers so I can inflict the same damage on him that he inflicted on me. But, I do not want to kill him, nor do I want to see him die."

In a last-ditch manoeuvre before Franklin was scheduled to die a federal judge put the Missouri death penalty on hold citing concerns involving the lethal drugs after receiving a lawsuit filed by Franklin and more then 15 other death-row inmates.

The state planned to be the first to use Propofol for executions, but Governor Jay Nixon reversed the decision based on a warning from the European Union whose members prohibited capital punishment and that they might halt shipments of the drug, leading to deficiencies for medical purposes. He ordered the Department of Corrections to come up with an alternative plan after backlash from the medical community who opposed the use of the surgical aesthetic for executions.

The Department of Corrections turned to pentobarbital, but Franklin's lawyers argued the deadly injection would violate the Constitution's ban on what was considered cruel and unusual punishment.

On November 19, U.S. District Judge Nanette Laughrey granted a stay of execution, based on the fact that Franklin's attorneys were able to show that the use of pentobarbital carried "a high risk of contamination and prolonged, unnecessary pain beyond that which is required to achieve death." While another federal judge granted a second stay based on a defense petition questioning Franklin's competency. U.S. District Judge Carol Jackson concluded that "a stay of execution is required to permit a meaningful review."

The State of Missouri appealed the two stays in the 8th U.S. Circuit Court of Appeals, which decided that Franklin's attorneys hadn't provided enough evidence to warrant a stay but the Federal Appellate Court overturned the U.S. District Court's decision.

The U.S. Supreme Court denied Franklin's request to halt the execution citing the present method of execution, lethal injection, was constitutionally allowable leading the way for the state executions to resume sealing his fate.

Joseph Paul Franklin was finally executed on November 20, 2013, after his death sentence was delayed for six hours due to court appeals. He refused a final meal and didn't give a final statement. With his long straggly hair pushed behind his ears and wearing black framed glasses, he was administered an injection of pentobarbital at 6:07 a.m. (CT) and died ten minutes later in the Potosi Correctional Center in Bonne Terre. He was the 35th inmate executed in the U.S. and the first in Missouri in almost three years.

In an interview with the St. Louis Post-Dispatch newspaper three days earlier Franklin said he had renounced his racist beliefs and partially blamed his motivation for his crimes on his abusive childhood.

At the end of this murderous rampage, he had robbed 16 banks, suspected in 22 murders in 11 states, confessed to 17 and was convicted of 8 known murders. He would later say his self-driven hate mission was to push his fellow supremacists to jump into action. But that never happened.

Gov. Jay Nixon said in a written statement that "the cowardly and calculated shootings outside a St. Louis-area synagogue were part of Joseph Paul Franklin's long record of murders and other acts of extreme violence across the country, fueled by religious and racial hate."

The 63-year-old escape artist, diagnosed paranoid schizophrenic and organized visionary serial killer, a man filled with so much hate and rage, had managed to elude law enforcement for years leaving in his wake dozens of grieving family members and friends including his only child, his daughter Lori who was only twelve months old when her father was arrested.

Although she had known he had committed crimes, she chose not to look up the particulars until she was 18 years old. Nor did she attend her father's execution. As a teenage mother, she had her own troubled life including growing up in poverty as well as having an alcohol problem much like her father and grandfather.

Despite her father's crimes, she often had prayed for a miracle that would have spared his life so he could have the chance to meet and get to know his great granddaughter even if it was through the glass barricade of the prison's visiting room.

Sources

Adams, Brook. "Mormon faith brought serial killer to Utah". The Salt Lake Tribune. November 18, 2013. http://archive.sltrib.com/story.php?ref=/sltrib/news/57102336-78/franklin-shot-race-fields.html.csp

Brauer, Sam, Bruch, Ryan A., Beonois, Ashleigh. "James Clayton Vaughn Jr. AKA Joseph Paul Franklin". Radford University. http://maamodt.asp.radford.edu/Psyc%20405/serial%20killers/Franklin,%20Joseph%20Paul.pdf

Clark Prosecutor.org. http://www.clarkprosecutor.org/html/death/US/franklin1355.htm

FBI. "Serial Killers Part 4: White Supremacist Joseph Franklin". https://www.fbi.gov/news/stories/2014/january/serial-killers-part-4-joseph-paul-franklin

Flynt, Larry. "Larry Flynt: Don't Execute the Man Who Paralyzed Me". The Hollywood Reporter. October 17, 2013. http://www.hollywoodreporter.com/news/larry-flynt-dont-execute-man-649158

Gaines, James R. People. "On the Trail of a Murderous Sniper Suspect: The Tangled Life of Joseph Paul Franklin". November 24, 1980. http://

www.people.com/people/archive/
article/0,,20077938,00.html

Lah, Kyung. "Serial killer Joseph Paul Franklin prepares to die". CNN. November 19, 2013. http://www.cnn.com/2013/11/18/justice/death-row-interview-joseph-paul-franklin/

Mungin, Lateef. "Serial killer Joseph Franklin executed after hours of delay". CNN. November 21, 2013. http://www.cnn.com/2013/11/20/justice/missouri-franklin-execution/

Murderpedia. http://murderpedia.org/male.F/f/franklin-joseph.htm

Nye, James and Gorman, Ryan and Associated Press Reporter. Daily Mail Online. "Neo Nazi serial killer Joseph Paul Franklin executed after Supreme Court overturns last-minute appeal over injection drug". November 20, 2013. http://www.dailymail.co.uk/news/article-2510543/Joseph-Paul-Franklin-serial-killer-paralyzed-Larry-Flynt-executed.html

Reavy, Pat. Joseph Paul Franklin was 'full of hatred,' 'evil' in 1980, attorney says".
Deseret News. November 20, 2013. http://www.deseretnews.com/article/865590976/Joseph-Paul-Franklin-was-full-of-hatred-evil-in-1980-attorney-says.html?pg=all

Terry, Don. Southern Poverty Law Center. November 20, 2013. https://www.splcenter.org/

hatewatch/2013/11/20/joseph-franklin-prolific-racist-serial-killer-executed

CHAPTER FOUR

Carol Bundy and Doug Clark

By the later 70's, the murder rate in the City of Angels had reached an all-time high, due to a number of serial killers at large. The Hillside Stranglers had been arrested for a rash of murders from 1977-1978, an unknown killer was targeting men on Skid Row, and since 1972 someone had killed and dumped over 40 young men along the highway just south of the city. Numerous other slayers remained unidentified and were at large.

With area homicide resources stretched to the limit, it appeared the police were in need of a miracle. Famous for its active nightlife for decades, Sunset Boulevard in West Hollywood has been illustrious over the years for much more. The area known as the "Sunset Strip", between Gardner Street and Western Avenue during the 70's and 80's was a magnet for drugs, street prostitution, and deadly secrets—even serial murder.

Carol Mary Bundy was born on August 26, 1942. Rejected by her mother and peers at school, she began to act out. By the age of 11 she was shop-lifting on a regular basis and made multiple attempts on her life by ingesting various poisons. Her first exposure with death would forever be imprinted in her mind—looking on as a young girl as her father hacked the heads off live chickens, their lifeless bodies flopping around in the dirt.

On the night of her mother's funeral when Carol was 14, her father forced her to perform oral sex on him. Less than a year after her mother's death, her father remarried and Carol began parading the streets at night naked, masturbating regularly and developed lesbian tendencies. Unable to control her, her father sent her away to live in numerous foster homes. When she was 17, she married a man almost 40 years her senior. By the time Carol met Doug Clark at the age of 37, she had just escaped a third marriage. After leaving her abusive husband, with whom she had two sons, she began having an affair with the manager of her apartment block, Jack Murray. When numerous attempts to bribe Murray's wife into leaving him failed, Bundy was evicted from her apartment. Yet her infatuation with the country singer continued, and she followed Murray to various venues where he was performing. It was at the country-western bar, Little Nashville, where Carol Bundy first met Doug Clark.

◆ ◆ ◆

Born on March 10, 1948, Douglas Daniel Clark was the son of a retired Naval Intelligence officer, Franklin Clark. In 1958, his father left the Navy for a civilian position as an engineer with the Transport Company of Texas. By the time Clark settled in Southern California, he'd lived in over 37 countries. He was polished, confident and well-educated. Clark referred to himself as "the king of the one-night stands," having kinky sex with underage girls and young women. He also had dark fantasies of rape, murder, mutilation and necrophilia, hoping for the day when his dreams would become reality. Clark realized that unattractive women were an easy mark because he could freely manipulate them into getting whatever he wanted. He had lived with several such women who paid the rent and bought clothing for him. The moment that their money ran out, he left them heartbroken and penniless.

Clark needed a new meal ticket, and it wouldn't be long before he set his sights on Carol. Winning her over wasn't difficult. He swept her off her feet and moved into her apartment the same night they had met. By day he worked in the boiler room of Jergens—a Burbank soap factory—and devoted his nights to perverse sexual experimentation with Carol. Still, nothing seemed to satisfy Doug. He wanted to fulfil his dark desires of capturing a girl and torturing her. At first, Carol didn't make much of his ramblings, believing they were nothing more than abnormal male fantasies. But as time went by, the thought of killing sounded like an exciting adventure.

In April 1980, Carol purchased two Raven .25-caliber automatic pistols at a pawnshop in Van Nuys. On the previous day, Doug had gone to the pawnshop and selected the guns he wanted, and then sent her to buy them. He told her that he was an ex-felon, having committed an armed robbery, and was therefore unable to purchase the guns himself.

Clark kept the nickel Raven pistol, while the chrome Raven was Carol's gun. Soon their killing spree would begin...

On June 12, 1980 at about 1:30 PM, police were called to a freeway ramp near the Forest Lawn Hollywood Hills Cemetery. While picking up trash, a highway worker had made a horrifying discovery—the bodies of two young girls. The following day, the remains were identified by the girls' distraught father, Angelo Marano of Huntington Beach. Along with his wife, he had been searching for them for almost a day and a half when he'd seen the news report and rushed to the police station. The girls, both high-school students, were known to have run away on previous occasions.

Gina Marano, age 15 was laying face down on the embankment. She was clothed only in a red tube-top which had been yanked down around her waist. Gina's half sister, Cynthia Chandler, a blond

16-year-old, was discovered with a pink jumpsuit wrapped around her legs. One leg of the jumpsuit was slit to the crotch as if there had been possible sexual activity. There was blood on the jumpsuit, and a stain which appeared to be grease or oil. No underwear was found on or near the bodies.

Investigators surmised from the crime scene that the girls were likely killed elsewhere, before their bodies were dumped down the hill and left in the baking sun. They had been there only a short time, in an open area for everyone to see, as if the killer couldn't care less if they were found—an MO similar to the Hillside Stranglers who had been caught just a year before.

According to the coroner's examination, Gina was killed by two gunshots to the head. Both bullets had exited her skull. Cynthia had been shot in the head and in the heart. The chest wound was deemed a contact shot, meaning the muzzle of the firearm was pressed against the body at the moment of discharge. Two .25 caliber bullets were recovered during the autopsy. It was estimated that the girls had been dead for at least 12 hours at the time their bodies were recovered, meaning that they were probably killed sometime on June 11, or up to approximately 4 AM on June 12. Lividity on Cynthia Chandler's body was consistent with the body having been moved from one location to another after death. The absence of puddles of blood and postmortem abrasions or scratches on her body confirmed that the girls had been killed elsewhere. Examination of vaginal samples taken from Cynthia contained spermatozoa. Although there was no evidence that Gina had been sexual assaulted, the possibility could not be ruled out, as bruising would not have resulted from post-mortem sexual penetration.

Soon after the murders, police received a phone call from an unidentified woman claiming her boyfriend had been involved in the killing of the teenagers. Unfortunately, the switchboard operator cut the female caller off believing she was a crank. While the unusual heat wave continued and spiked across Los Angeles, 11 days passed since the discovery of the bodies and the police had no solid leads.

On the afternoon of June 23, an officer patrolling Sunset Boulevard met a prostitute named Karen Jones and warned her not to be milling about in the area. At around 3:15 AM, Jones' body was discovered on Franklin Avenue laying next to the curb in a pool of blood. The cause of death—a gunshot wound to the head. A .25-caliber jacketed bullet was also retrieved during the autopsy. The coroner estimated that the gun had been fired six to twelve inches from the victim's head. He was unable to determine whether she had engaged in sexual activity in the hours leading up to her death. It's believed that Karen Jones was killed between midnight and 2 AM, on June 23.

Early that same morning, a naked decapitated body was discovered in the parking lot of the Studio City Sizzler in Burbank beside a metal trash bin. Inside the dumpster was a red dress with a sash cut into pieces which authorities believed belonged to 25-year-old Exxie Wilson—a veteran prostitute, and friend of Karen Jones. No other clothing or personal belongings were found at the scene. Though the police searched the area exhaustively, the victim's head was nowhere to be found.

Four days later, at 1 AM on June 27, Jonathan Caravello discovered an ornate wooden box with an oversized lid. It had been left in the alley on Hoffman Street behind his apartment, only a block from a busy intersection. Excited and hoping the chest contained something valuable, he parked his car and went to check it out. Unlatching the lid, he was shocked to discover the severed head of Exxie Wilson, wrapped in blue jeans and a pink T-shirt with the inscription, "Daddy's Girl." These items of clothing would later be identified as belonging to another victim. Horrified, Caravello ran from the scene and immediately contacted police.

The coroner determined that, in all likelihood, the head had been removed after death. Still, he admitted that it was possible that the victim might have been unconscious or dying at the time. At least 15 to 20 cuts were used to complete the decapitation. The head had been frozen and appeared to have been scrubbed clean. At the time, no one knew why. The official cause of death was a single gunshot to the back of the head. Once again, a .25-caliber jacketed bullet was recovered from the skull. Vaginal samples from Wilson's body all contained spermatozoa.

Assistant Chief of Investigation, James Kono told the Associated Press, "We have examined the body and the neck…and the wounds all match up." Ballistics analysis revealed that the bullet recovered from the head was fired from a Raven—the same weapon used to kill the stepsisters as well as Karen Jones. Jones was found about three miles from where Exxie Wilson had been dumped, and about two miles from where the stepsister's bodies were found.

After the discovery of Exxie Wilson's head, newspapers were claiming that a new "Sunset Strip Slayer" was on the loose. The City of Angels had another serial killer on their hands—one that was committing two murders at a time.

At a press conference in the Parker Center at the Los Angeles Police Department, authorities were tight-lipped, refusing to discuss details of their investigation. Instead, they asked the public for information and urged any anonymous callers who had contacted the police earlier to call again, promising their names and personal details would be kept confidential.

Lt. Ron Lewis stated to the *Los Angeles Times* that Jones and Wilson were from Little Rock, Arkansas. They had been in the city for about two weeks with their pimp, "Albright", who had been questioned and was not a suspect. Lt. Lewis did say that Wilson's head had probably been placed in the alley a few hours before Jonathan Caravello found it, which led the media to believe that a particularly depraved killer had kept the head for days.

On June 30, the nude remains of a young woman were found partially hidden under an old mattress by snake hunters in a ravine off Foothill Boulevard, north of the Golden State Freeway in the San Fernando Valley. The coroner estimated the victim's age as between 17 and 25 and added that she was approximately 5'7". She had been dead for 90-120 days. Her skin was mummified making her the first victim in the series of five. The autopsy revealed she had suffered three gunshot wounds to the chest. Two .25-caliber jacketed bullets were recovered from the body and linked to the other murders. She was identified as Marnette Comer (a.k.a. Annette Ann Davis)—a blond prostitute from Sacramento. Sabra Comer, the victim's sister, said she had last seen Marnette on May 21. At the time, she was wearing a pink T-shirt with the words "Daddy's Girl" printed on it, just like the one found wrapped around Exxie Wilson's head.

As fear spread across the city that more

victims may turn up, authorities held another press conference. Detectives decided to display the crudely made pine box in which Exxie Wilson's head was found and allowed the press to photograph it in hopes that someone would recognize the brass ring decorations and metal border. "We believe the killer is someone from this area," said Detective Sergeant John Helvin, "but we don't know for sure."

Meanwhile, with help from the public, the box was traced to a Texas manufacturer, Chicago Arts, an importer/distributor of Mexican-made boxes. Detectives scrambled to follow up on the lead.

With the heat wave lingering over Los Angeles like a heavy smog, the serial killer's pattern suddenly changed. This time the victim was male and would never have been linked to the series if it wasn't for a phone call on August 11 from a woman claiming to have murdered him.

The body had been found inside his van on Barbara Ann Street on August 9, approximately five days after he had been killed. His skin was blistered, his corpse bloated and decomposing from being in the vehicle in the scalding heat. Like Exxie Wilson, he had been decapitated, and his head was missing. He had been stabbed nine times and sliced across his buttocks to his anus. Shell casings were also found at the scene, but without the head, investigators weren't sure if he had been shot or not.

Police identified the victim as John "Jack"

Robert Murray, 45, of Van Nuys, a tall and handsome, smooth-talking country singer who had worked part-time at Little Nashville, a bar located a few blocks from where his body was discovered.

The caller was Carol Bundy, an overweight matronly 37-year-old vocational nurse who worked at Valley Medical Center in Van Nuys. She stated that she was involved with a man, Douglas Clark, who was the "Sunset Strip Slayer". The police arrested Bundy at her home and seized three pairs of panties belonging to the victims, along with an album containing photographs of Clark in compromising positions with an 11-year-old girl. Once Carol Bundy started talking there was no stopping her. The story she told was one of rape, murder and post-mortem sex.

Carol confessed to killing Murray herself because after she had helped Clark get rid of Exxie Wilson's head, she had confided in Murray. Terrified that he would tell the police, she shot him in the head and stabbed him numerous times in the back. Fearing the bullets would be traced back to her, she decided to decapitate him with a boning knife—not an easy task, but she got the job done. She also stated that Doug had helped her dispose of Murray's head, which was never found.

Doug Clark was arrested for his possible involvement in Jack Murray's murder and was also questioned about the Sunset Strip Slayings.

Following the arrest of Bundy and Clark,

another body was found on August 26, 1980 near the Sierra Highway in Antelope Valley. A worker inspecting water towers stumbled upon human bones scattered in a 10' radius around an oily spot that reeked of decomposing flesh. A cluster of blond hair was found in the vicinity where the remains were discovered. The victim, an unidentified young female known as "Jane Doe 18" had died about one to two months earlier. The official cause of death: a gunshot wound to the back of the head. A .25-caliber jacketed bullet was recovered from the temporal area of the skull.

Two days later, the mummified remains of "Jane Doe 99" were found down an embankment in a remote area near Malibu known as Tuna Canyon. The victim was wearing a black tank top and skirt, both wrapped around her waist. Deputies also found a clump of blond hair below where the body was found which appeared to belong to the victim. The coroner's examination showed that Jane Doe 99 was 5'3", with blond hair and was approximately 20 years old. She had been killed by a gunshot wound to the left forehead. Ballistics examination of bullet fragments taken from the skull revealed that they had come from a .25-caliber ACP bullet jacket. The characteristics of these bullet fragments generally matched those of the bullet found in the skull of yet another Jane Doe, this one numbered 28, but there were too few fragments to make a positive ballistics identification.

A prostitute, known as Charlene A.*, was working on Sunset Boulevard at about 10 PM, on April 27, 1980, when a man driving a blue Buick station wagon solicited her for oral sex. After she got into the car, the man began stabbing her in the back, neck, arms, chest and stomach. As she struggled, Charlene grabbed the knife by the blade, severing the tendons in her hand. At one point, she said, "Mister, that's blood. You're hurtin' me." He laughed and said, "I know." Eventually she was able to escape her attacker and would later identify the man in court as being Doug Clark.

During interrogation by police, Clark freely admitted he had visited the Hollywood area on a regular basis trolling for prostitutes. He stated he sometimes would go alone, but on numerous occasions he went with Carol. He claimed on one night, he and Bundy "cruised" Anaheim after reading news stories of the Sunset Strip killings because they wanted to see other areas where prostitutes hang out. Occasionally, they paid hookers for "threesomes."

He admitted to detectives that his mother knew that he'd "been a little weird for a long time. She caught me dressed in her and my sister's underwear when I was nine years old." He had also "started into damn near everything" when he was in the ninth grade in Switzerland, "[a]nd since then I've never been able to look at sex just straight on. It had to be kinky…"

Clark continued by saying he knew "about 100 whores" since he lived in Los Angeles, and that it was "important to be able to have a conversation with a prostitute." He denied any interest in necrophilia, but Carol would tell a different tale about an afternoon while her sons were visiting relatives. According to Bundy, Clark removed Exxie Wilson's severed head from the refrigerator and placed it on the kitchen counter. "We had a lot of fun with her [head]. Where I had my fun was with the makeup. I was making her over like a big Barbie doll…", Bundy once told a magazine reporter. After Carol made the head more physically appealing as a sex toy, Doug took his prized trophy into the shower and had necrophilic oral sex with it.

Originally Clark was charged with the six counts of murder, three counts of sexual misconduct against a minor, and one count of being an accessory after the fact to the murder of Jack Murray because he had aided Bundy in disposing of Murray's decapitated head. The preliminary hearing on the charges began on October 20, 1980. An additional count of mutilation of human remains was added at his arraignment in November 13, 1980.

But what the police and prosecutors needed more than anything was Carol Bundy on their side. And they were willing to make her a deal in exchange for her testimony against Doug Clark.

By the time opening statements began before a jury of four men and eight women, Clark would be tried on the six murder counts, one count of mutilation of human remains, and the Charlene A. attempted murder and mayhem count. The charges involving a minor, (Shannon O) were severed, and the prosecutor withdrew the charge of accessory after the fact to the murder of Jack Murray due to Carol Bundy's confession to the murder.

The courtroom was packed with television reporters, journalists and curious onlookers. The testimony would take four months and was described by Deputy District Attorney Rober Jorgensen as "an intimate tour of a sewer." He also called, Clark a "cowardly butcher of little girls" and a necrophiliac.

The defense would portray Clark as articulate, an intelligent man with an above-average IQ of 118 and that the case against him was only circumstantial. Clark quickly make himself look like an arrogant fool by "calling the court officers names and disrupting the proceedings with temper tantrums." It was clear from the get-go that Clark's strategy from the time he was arrested was to blame Bundy for everything.

Arrogant and acting in his own defense at times during the trial with his court-appointed lawyers, he claimed he was innocent and was clearly duped by the woman and her lover, Jack Murray, who had plotted to frame him for the Sunset murders.

During Carol Bundy's testimony, she was dressed like the housewife next door, prim and proper-like, and spoke of being under Clark's spell. She also talked about how Doug had brought home the head of one victim and how he had bragged about "committing murders since he was 17-years-old—to the tune of about 47 [victims]".

Besides the prosecution's star witness, Clark's fingerprints were on the murder weapon which had been found hidden at his place of employment. Furthermore, Dr. Gloria Keyes—a forensic psychiatrist—testified that he had "antisocial personality disorder." All told, Doug Clark didn't have a chance in hell of winning over the jury and proving his innocence. Other diagnoses presented at the trial included psychosexual disorders, shared paranoia, and possibly an atypical psychosis. Keyes believed his psychosexual disorder was "paraphilia, including fetishism, pedophilia, and the acting out of fantasies". She went on to testify that Doug Clark was "sane" and he "intended to commit the killings."

Five days after the jury deliberated on January 28, 1983, Doug Clark was found guilty of six counts of murder and one count of the attempted murder of Charlene A. On March 16, 1983, he received six death sentences and was sentenced to serve his time at San Quentin where he continues to sit on California's death row alongside Lawrence Bittaker, Randy Kraft and an assortment of other serial killers.

After Carol Bundy's initial confession, she planned on pleading "not guilty of murder by reason of insanity" in the murder of Jack Murray and "assisting in the murder" of an unidentified prostitute (Jane Doe 28), but changed her mind at the last minute before her trial was scheduled to begin on May 2, 1983.

"It was really fun to do," she admitted and acknowledged that she would probably do it again. Realizing her comments regarding murdering Murray would make her look bad, she decided to accept a plea deal—one which would spare her from the death penalty.

On May 31, she received consecutive prison terms of 25 year-to-life on the count of participating in the murder of Jane Doe 28 and 27 years-to-life for the murder of Jack Murray and the use of an illegal firearm. She was sentenced to the California Institution for Women at Frontera and was deemed eligible for parole in 2012.

While incarcerated she continued to be in contact with Clark, even urging him to use her, by way of her psychiatric files that she had handed over to his lawyer, to free himself. Carol Bundy died of heart failure on December 9, 2003 at the age of 61.

From behind bars, Clark continued to proclaim his innocence and petitioned the court for a new trial. His request was dismissed.

In June 1992 the California Supreme Court confirmed his death sentence. Ever the lady's man, Clark married Kelly Keniston, a woman who helped him in his pursuit to prove his innocence.

Mark MacNamara, a journalist with over 25 years experience, both as a staff writer and freelancer for newspapers and magazines, including *Vanity Fair*, discussed interviews he had conducted with Carol Bundy and Doug Clark on Larry King Live. MacNamara was uncertain about Clark's involvement in the murders: "In many respects he is not a likable person: He exhibits many of the characteristics of a sociopath: he lies and has a grandiose vision of himself, for example. He is also a satyr. But did he kill these prostitutes. In fact, he had frequented prostitutes for years, and seemed to flourish in the sexual underworld of swing clubs and street sex. 'I had been going to prostitutes for years,' he often told me. 'I liked prostitutes. Why didn't I kill any of those girls' Of course, one could argue that it wasn't until he met Bundy that he fell into a *folie a deux*, which drew him over the edge of sexual experimentation."

There are still many people who believe that Carol Bundy was the manipulative mastermind behind all the murders—that it was her depraved need to please Clark that fed into his sexual perversion. Regardless of whose story you choose to believe, one thing is certain, Carol Bundy and Doug Clark were truly a match made in Hell.

Sources

Haines, Max. "Haines: Deadly Desires." The Sudbury Star. July 7, 2012.
http//www.thesudburystar.com/2012/07/07/haines-deadly-desires

Murderpedia. "Carol Mary Bundy."

Newton, Michael. The Encyclopedia of Serial Killers. New York: Checkmark Books, 2000.

Ramsland, Katherine. "Love and Death: The Sunset Strip Killers."
http://www.trutv.com/library/crime/serial_killers/partners/cbundy/11.html

Stanford Law School. People v. Clark (1992) 3 Cal.4th 41, 10 Cal.
Rptr.2d 554; 833 P.2d 561.

CHAPTER FIVE

Fred and Rosemary West

On February 24, 1994, *"Things Can Only Get Better"* by D: Ream was racing to the top of the UK dance-pop song charts. Little did the British public know that things were about to get much worse. At an average three-storey brick house in central Gloucester, secrets hidden for decades were about to be unearthed; abuse, incest, paedophilia, depravity, torture, rape, and murder. On that damp and bitterly cold Thursday afternoon, a van filled with four police officers arrived at 25 Cromwell Street at 1:45 PM looking for the owner, Fred West. They were greeted by his stocky wife, Rosemary. At that moment an officer handed her a warrant to dig up their garden, she yelled to her eldest son, Steve, "Get Fred! They're going to dig up the garden, looking for Heather."

While Rose continued to scream hysterically for her husband, an hour passed and still there was no sign of Fred West, even though a phone message was left at his workplace at Carson

Contractors. In the meantime, a small group of officers dressed in blue protective overalls began lifting the heavy patio slabs at the bottom of the garden. When Steve was finally able to get a hold of his father by cell phone, Fred was eerily calm. He told his frantic son not to worry—that he was on his way. At 4 PM, daylight faded, and large lamps were brought in to illuminate the garden. As the police team used a small mechanical digger and dug a hole at the furthest point from the house, Rose and the older children kept watch from an upstairs window. After searching for about an hour and finding nothing but a chicken bone, work stopped at the site for the day. When Fred arrived home just before 6 PM, he offered no explanation as to where he had been. Had he spent the last four hours contemplating the situation and how he was going to handle it?

He decided to drive to the police department where he spoke with Hazel Savage, a veteran Detective Constable who was experienced in investigations involving women and children. The dark-haired, man complained that the police were harassing him, wanting to put him back in prison on another "false charge". He said that he and his wife, Rose, had no idea where Heather was. "Lots of girls disappear," he explained, "take a different name and go into prostitution." He claimed that Heather was a lesbian who had some major problems with drugs.

Meanwhile, Rose was being interviewed back

at the house, and told a very similar story. Heather had disappeared in 1987 at the age of 16. According to Rose, the young girl had run away before. She described her daughter as "difficult" and repeated the story about Heather being a lesbian.

The next morning, fearing that the police would find his daughter's remains, Fred admitted to Constable Savage that he had "killed her." When he arrived at the police station, he described in detail how he had cut Heather's body into three pieces and buried them, repeating over and over that Rose had known nothing about the murder. Then, less than a half hour later, he changed his story and denied everything.

"Heather's alive and well, right. She's possibly in Bahrain working for a drug cartel. She had a Mercedes, a chauffeur, and a new birth certificate." He assured the police they could dig all they wanted, but they would not find her.

As dawn stretched across Gloucester, the team of diggers, now dressed in bright yellow overalls with their hoods raised against the pouring rain, returned to resume their work in hopes of finding Heather West. It wouldn't be long before they unearthed what they were looking for—and more than they ever imagined.

After several hours of digging failed to produce Heather's grave, the police decided to broaden the search area. While exploring another spot near the back door of the house close to the old church wall, the officers stumbled upon what appeared to be a piece of human bone. But since Gloucester was built on Roman burial grounds and the fact that the bone was discovered alone and away from the original search area, it wasn't deemed important enough to move from the main digging site at the back of the garden. Later that afternoon, a second hole was excavated on the left side of the patio near some fir trees. Two feet down, a team member spotted a large brown object. After Professor Knight, a scientist, cautiously washed the muck from the object, he identified it as a femur—discolored from years of being buried in the ground. The freshly dug pit stank of death, the smell swirling in a revolving bouquet of decomposing human flesh and bodily organs mixed within the dirt. Upon closer inspection, the searchers discovered a heap of bones in a small cavity less than a foot across. Under the ribs were fragments of a black bin bag and large teeth; clumps of hair lay not far from a skull. They also recovered fingernails and two lengths of rope.

Back at Gloucester police department, the bones were examined by Professor Knight. He confirmed that they belonged to a young woman who had been dismembered and decapitated prior to being buried. Knight noted that it was odd that the kneecaps and several bones from the hands and foot were missing. Later that day, it was established that the bone shard found by the back door of the house was indeed human and did not belong to the main skeleton of the young woman. It was then that the police realized there might be more than one body buried in the Wests' garden...

Fredrick Walter Stephen West was born to Walter and Daisy West on September 29, 1941 in Much Marcle—a small town nestled in the Herefordshire countryside, surrounded by green pastures, golden cornfields, and apple orchards. Having lost a baby girl who had been born prematurely the year before, Walter and Daisy were thrilled to behold their beautiful baby boy, with his straw-yellow hair and eyes the color of sapphires.

Over the next decade, Daisy would give birth to six more children; John, David (who died a month after birth from a heart defect), Elizabeth (known as Little Daisy), Douglas, Kitty, and Gwen.

Out of all the children, Fred was Daisy's favorite and her pride toward the little boy was evident to everyone in the community. Over time, it would cause jealousy and fights among the other children. To her, little Freddie was precious. She would take him to bed with her every night, cuddling and caressing him. To most people, the bond between Fred and Daisy seemed "unnatural". According to Daisy's sister-in-law, Edna Hill, "Fred came first with Daisy, even in front of Walter."

In July 1946, the family moved back to Moorcourt Cottage where Fred had been born. They lived in immense poverty without electricity or gas and with toilet facilities consisting of nothing more than a bucket. As Fred grew, he inherited his mother's ample mouth along with a gap between his front teeth. His hair turned from blond to dark brown with bushy unkempt curls. During his school years, he was not considered a particularly bright student, and was constantly in trouble. On many occasions, his mother would march into the schoolhouse and scream at his teacher for disciplining her pride and joy. Because of her routine involvement, the other students would mock and bully him. According to his younger brother, Doug, Fred was "mammy's blue-eyed boy" and could do no wrong, as she always took Fred's side in squabbles involving the other children. As a result of Daisy's coddling, Fred grew to be a spoilt and introverted child.

With the West family cut off from the rest of the world, rumors ran rampant that Daisy had taken Fred into her bed when he was 12 and seduced him. Gossip of deviant sex was not unheard of deep within the rolling hills of the Herefordshire countryside. Walter was the most prevailing influence upon Fred's emerging sexuality by allegedly teaching the small scruffy boy who reeked of pigs how to have sex with sheep at the age of 8-years-old.

Much later in life, Fred spoke often about

his father's sexual appetites, claiming Walter had engaged in sex with children. Fred claimed Walter openly discussed having sex with his young daughters, using the logic, "I made you so I'm entitled to have you". It's unsurprising that Fred would grow up with the same mentality, maintaining that "everyone did it".

At the age of 15, Fred left school, barely literate, and found work as a farm hand. Within a year he began shaving regularly and dressing in clean clothes. He became exceedingly aggressive with the opposite sex, chasing after any girl who caught his eye, engaging in sex games, and not caring about the identity or age of the girls involved; behavior which would follow him into adulthood.

On the evening of November 28, 1958, Fred was riding his motorcycle, a James 125, when the 17-year-old was seriously injured in an accident a few hundred yards from home. He would spend a week in a coma. The crash left him with lacerations, broken bones, and forced the doctors to fit a metal plate into his head to keep his shattered skull together. His leg was smashed to pieces and had to be held together with a metal brace until the bones healed. The experience would leave him with a crooked nose, one leg shorter than the other, and a propensity to fly into uncontrollable fits of rage.

After recovering from his injuries, Fred met Catherine Bernadette Costello—nicknamed Rena—an attractive 16-year-old prostitute and accomplished thief. They became lovers quickly but the affair ended a few months later when Rena returned to her native Scotland. With Rena long gone, Fred turned his attention to a young woman at a local youth club. When he shoved his hand up her skirt, she knocked him off the fire escape and sent him tumbling to the ground below where he smacked his head and lost consciousness. Months later, he was accused of getting a friend of the West family, a 13-year-old girl, pregnant. Even worse, he didn't see anything unusual, wrong, or shocking with molesting young girls, something he had been doing since his early teens. "Well, doesn't everyone do it?"

Disgusted by Fred's behaviour, Daisy ordered him to find somewhere else to live. His mother's rejection marked a huge turning point in Fred's life, and was the cause of great bitterness between him and Daisy. He was sent to live with his mother's sister, Violet, where he went to work on various construction projects. But it wasn't long before he was stealing from the construction sites and having sex with young girls. Even one of his underage former girlfriends, who lived in Newent, claimed that Fred had raped her on two occasions.

During his trial for having intercourse with the 13-year-old, Fred's doctor contended that his deviant behaviour was due to epileptic fits caused by a possible brain injury from either his fall or the motorcycle accident. As a result, Fred escaped a jail sentence, but was convicted as a child molester and petty thief shortly after his twentieth birthday.

In 1962, at the request of his mother, Fred moved back with his family at the Moorcourt Cottage in Much Marcle. It was also the summer that Rena Costello returned from Scotland pregnant by a Pakistani bus driver. Later that year, Fred and Rena were secretly married. In March of 1963, Rena gave birth to Charmaine. To hide the fact that the child was of Asian descent, Fred and Rena concocted a plan to tell Daisy that the baby had died in childbirth, so they had decided to adopt a mixed-race child.

Despite the fact that Rena was an occasional prostitute, she was becoming exceedingly unhappy about her husband's ravenous and abnormal sexual appetite. "He wanted oral sex, bondage and sodomy at all hours of the day and night." With his new job driving an ice cream truck, Fred discovered he had unlimited access to many teenage girls which afforded him almost daily sexual escapades.

In 1964, Rena gave birth to Fred's child, a daughter they named Anne Marie. She was given the middle name Kathleen Daisy, in honor of Fred's mother. She would grow up to have the Wests' family features; blue eyes, a broad nose, pale skin, and wiry dark brown hair. While Fred doted on his first child, Anna Marie, Charmaine received only criticism and was the brunt of his bad temper. Sometimes he caged her like an animal for hours on end. Over the next several years, Fred and Rena's marriage was described as an "on again, off again" relationship, filled with insecurity, jealousy and infidelity. One of Fred's monumental affairs was with a 22-year-old woman who worked in a bottled water factory nearby. She became pregnant by Fred and gave birth in July 1966 to a son, Steven. Howard Sounes, the author of *Fred and Rose*, said, "there was also evidence that another of Fred's Scottish girlfriends became pregnant by him, and they had a son named Gareth". No one really knows for sure how many children Fred West fathered, since he was having affairs with numerous women at the same time. It was during this period that Fred and Rena met Anna McFall, an attractive teenager whose boyfriend had been killed in an accident.

Fred was also involved in another accident of his own when he "accidentally" ran his ice cream truck over a 3-year old boy and killed him. Fearing he would lose his job after the incident, Fred and Rena packed up Charmaine and Anna Marie and moved to Gloucester where he started working at a slaughterhouse. According to author Colin Wilson, "One thing is clear: that at some stage, West developed a morbid obsession with corpses and blood and dismemberment. There is no evidence that he had shown any such interest so far. It seems, then, that Fred West's sexual perversion became slowly more obsessive in the period following his marriage, and the evidence suggests that necrophilia and desire to mutilate corpses began during his period as a butcher."

Fred and Rena's marriage became increasingly difficult and strained. In one instance of many, Fred slapped Rena in the face because his dinner wasn't ready on time. Rena wanted to take the two children back to Glasgow with her. When Fred refused, she returned to Scotland alone, worried sick that something might happen to them. In the summer of 1966, Rena returned to Gloucester to find Fred and Anna McFall living together in a trailer. Feeling betrayed and angry about Fred's relationship with Anna, Rena stole some of Anna's belongings. The theft was reported, and Rena traveled to Scotland in the hopes of evading police but was brought back to England by a young Gloucester detective named Hazel Savage.

Early in 1967, Anna McFall became pregnant with Fred's child and began pushing him to divorce Rena and marry her. In the final weeks of her pregnancy, when the stress of Anna's constant demands threatened the stability of his life, Fred killed her. Anna McFall was last seen in July 1967. It is believed that Fred used the skills he had learned at the slaughterhouse to dismember her corpse and bury her. When her remains were finally found, numerous small hand and foot bones were missing, as well as her ankle and wrist bones. It also appeared that Fred had sliced off her fingers and toes, possibly to make it more difficult to identify her, but more likely because it sexually excited him—giving him a feeling of power to keep her body parts as trophies. Nestled beside Anna's remains was the skeleton of her unborn child. The remains were buried in Finger Post Field, a place familiar to Fred. As her grave had been dug close to his home, some experts believe this gave Fred complete control over her, even in death. It would be 27 years before Anna McFall's remains would be discovered. It is not known if the foetus had been cut from her womb, but at the time, Fred had developed a bizarre interest in conducting abortions and even boasted to friends that he offered his services to carry out the terminations for teenage girls in a garage where he performed the work. He kept a large collection of odd instruments and supplies including an oxyacetylene burner, large knives, antiseptic, and a 10 inch tube with a corkscrew attached to the end.

Not long after Fred had murdered Anna, he moved to a house in Bishop's Cleeve. Rena moved back in with him and their relationship greatly improved. They took their children out of care and stayed together as a family for the remainder of the year. The Wests were very open about their sexual relationship. Rena began prostituting again for extra money and Fred sometimes showed friends pornographic photographs of his wife.

It was at this time, that Fred started fondling Charmaine by rubbing the half-naked child over his groin.

In January 1968, a pretty 15-year-old waitress, named Mary Bastholm who worked at the Pop-In cafe was abducted from a bus stop in Gloucester. Scotland Yard was called in and a major search was launched involving hundreds of officers scouring the ditches and fields in the area but the search was called off due to bad weather. Howard Sounes believes that Fred was responsible for Basholm's disappearance as Fred abducted other women in the same fashion often from bus stops years later. There were numerous links between Fred and Mary Bastholm; Fred was a customer at the cafe where Mary served him tea, Fred had been employed to do some building work behind the Pop-In, and Mary had been spotted with a woman fitting the description of Fred's former lover, Anna McFall. One witness also claimed to have seen the waitress in Fred's car.

When Fred's son, Stephen, visited his father in prison in 1995, Fred refused to tell him where the body of Mary Batholm was buried. Fred boasted, "They are not going to find them all, you know, never".

Stephen asked him, "Mary?" and claimed his father replied, "I will never tell anyone where she is". Her disappearance was never solved, her body never found.

♦ ♦ ♦

On February 6, Fred's mother died at the age of 44 due to complications arising from a gallbladder operation. Her death launched him into a cycle of petty thefts, and he frequently changed jobs. In November 1968, while working as a bakery delivery driver, Fred met the girl of his dreams, his next wife, soul mate, and partner in murder.

Rosemary Pauline Letts was born on November 29, 1953 in Devon, England. Her mother, Daisy Letts, suffered from severe depression and her father, Bill Letts was a paranoid schizophrenic and a violent domestic dictator who demanded obedience from his wife and children. He enjoyed disciplining the children and at times seemed to look for reasons to beat them. As a result of Bill's psychotic episodes, he drifted through various low-paying jobs which usually left his family short on money.

His son, Andrew, recalled just how much of a tyrant his father could be:

"If he felt we were in bed too late, he would throw a bucket of cold water over us. He would order us to dig the garden, and that meant the whole garden. Then he would inspect it like an army officer, and if he was not satisfied, we would have to do it all over again. We were not allowed to speak and play like normal children. If we were noisy, he would go for us with a

belt or chunk of wood. He would beat you black and blue until mum got in between us. Then she would get a good hiding".

After Daisy had given birth to three daughters and a son, she had a difficult time coping with her violent husband. Her depression deepened and resulted in hospitalization in 1953 where she was treated with electroshock therapy. Shortly after numerous gruelling treatments Daisy gave birth to Rosemary. It's unknown whether ECT treatments had any adverse effects on her newborn daughter. Given the damage ECT can do to the patient it seems extremely unlikely the foetus would remain unaffected.

For Rose, school was not a happy time. Overweight, an underachiever, and a rebel against authority, she was taunted by the other students. It wouldn't be long before she became the aggressor and would attack anyone who teased her. During her teenage years, she was sexually precocious. She would walk around the house partially clothed or naked depending on her mood. Occasionally, she would climb into her younger brother's bed and fondle him. Since the local boys her age gave her little attention, Rose focused on older man in the area. During this time, Rose claimed she had been raped twice by a man in the village.

When her parents split up early in 1969, Rose moved in with her mother and attended Cleeve

School. six months later, the 15-year-old decided to live with her father in Bishop's Cleave near Cheltenham, a move which surprised everyone. Rumors quickly circulated that Rose and her father were having an incestuous relationship, and that Bill Letts had a reputation for molesting young girls.

While waiting at a bus stop in Cheltenham, Rose met Fred West, a man 12 years older than her. He had striking blue eyes, wild dark curly hair much like a bird's nest, long bushy sideburns and he walked with a limp. With very few friends, Rose was flattered by his attention. Fred told Rose that his wife had left him with two small children to look after, and at times he could barely manage. But the truth was, Rena had left Fred and was living in Gloucester where she was found guilty of "attempting to defraud the Department of Social Security". As soon as Rose heard Fred had children, she instantly became fascinated with him and agreed to go to his home. Over the weeks that followed, Rose visited regularly and became a playmate for the two girls. Charmaine was now 6, (only 10 years younger than Rose), and Anne Marie was 5.

As they spent more time together, Rose noticed how Fred treated each of the girls differently. Anne Marie was "Dad's girl" and even told him she wanted to marry him one day. She had received all his attention, while his stepdaughter, Charmaine, was basically tolerated. In fact, there were times when Fred was outright cruel, beating Charmaine for absolutely no reason. If there was no woman around to look after the children, he ignored the girls' daily upkeep, and it was nothing for him to bundle them up and drive them to Social Services in Gloucester where they were put in temporary foster care. Because of the girls' ages, they should have been identified as vulnerable children, but Fred West was never scrutinized carefully enough. If he had been, maybe things would have been different.

Fred was thrilled to find someone to look after his children. He also found Rose sexually electrifying. His relationship with Rose blossomed into more than just a nanny to his children. She had graduated to a secret lover—much like Anna McFall.

By this time, Fred had developed depraved ideas about sex. He was excited by aggressive, sadistic sex and began accumulating sadomasochistic pornography. It was tough to find girls who didn't mind being tied up and beaten. He enjoyed giving punishment a much as receiving it. Rena had outright refused to be a part of Fred's sex games, but in Rose he found a more than willing partner. Fred introduced Rose to prostitution, and she began entertaining men at home. He was thankful for the extra money it brought in. He also enjoyed watching Rose through a spy-hole in the door while she was having sex with other men.

When Rose's father learned Rose was selling

her body for money, he went to Gloucester social services and suggested his underage daughter be taken away from Fred. In the summer of 1969, Rose was taken to a home for troubled teenagers where she continued to communicate with Fred. Once she reached her sixteenth birthday, the authorities would not be able to detain her and she would be free to return to her lover. Before she was to be discharged from the home, Fred was sent to prison for 30 days for various thefts and failing to pay fines. Again, Anne Marie and Charmaine were placed in foster care.

A few weeks later, Rose went back to live with her father until he learned that she was pregnant with Fred's child. Rose packed her bags and left her father's house to take care of Charmaine and Anne Marie.

◆ ◆ ◆

After Fred was released from prison, he gathered his children from foster care and moved his family to 25 Midland Road, a squalid semi-detached building divided into three flats in Gloucester in June of 1970. While his troubled marriage with Rena was over, she suddenly reappeared the following month and demanded that her girls be returned to her. Fred refused.

With Rose and two children to provide for and rent to pay, money was short, and Fred resorted to petty crime: stealing tires from one employer and a vehicle licence from another. He was stopped by police and arrested.

On October 17, Rose gave birth to her first child with Fred. They named her Heather Ann. She was a pretty baby with the same identifiable dark hair as the West family and facial features that resembled her mother. With three children to care for, constant money problems, and Fred in jail, Rose's temper exploded. More than anything, she resented having to take care of Rena's children, and treated them poorly. As the bleak winter months of the new year settled in, Rose's frustration grew. 17-years-old, a baby herself, she was unable to command respect or love from Anne Marie and Charmaine, so Rose beat them and plotted punishments as sadistic as her own father had used on her.

When a neighbor's child barged into Rose's kitchen one day, she found Charmaine standing on a kitchen chair with her hands tied behind her back with a leather belt. Rose held a long wooden spoon in her hand which was clearly being used to beat Charmaine. In another incident, when Charmaine was taking too long to wash up in the kitchen, Rose grabbed the child's cereal bowl from her hand and smashed it over Anne Marie's head.

In a letter written by Rose to Fred in prison, it was clear that Rose's hatred toward Charmaine, the high-spirited 8-year-old who wet the bed and dreamed of one day being rescued by her mother was growing.

"...Darling, about Char. I think she likes to be handled rough. But darling, why do I have to be the one to do it. I would keep her for her own sake, if it wasn't for the rest of the rest of the children. You can see Char coming out in Anne now. And I hate it."

Shortly after Rose and the children visited Fred in prison on June 15, 1971, Charmaine went missing. It is believed that while Anne Marie was at school, Rose lost her temper and either beat or stabbed Charmaine to death. As Rose faced questions from family, friends, and Anne Marie regarding the disappearance of Charmaine, Rose already had a story in place—that Charmaine's real mother, Rena, had taken her away to live with her in Bristol. This would be the same story Rose would tell repeatedly for the next 24 years.

On June 24, Fred was finally released from prison. When Rose gave him the news about Charmaine, he wasn't surprised—it wasn't as if the child was his. With his stepdaughter dead, now Fred and Rose had something in common, a secret that Fred would hold over Rose for the rest of her life.

Since Fred was in jail when Charmaine was murdered his involvement was probably limited to disposing and burying her body.

Despite their silent pact, Rose decided to pack up baby Heather and leave Fred, the strain of her crime too much as people kept asking about

Charmaine's whereabouts. Rose moved back in with her father at Tobyfield Road and told him that she was done with Fred. That same day, Fred showed up at the house and begged her to come home, "Come on Rosie, you know what we've got between us." He also stated, if she wasn't back home in 10 minutes, her place in his bed would be filled with another woman. This seemed to upset Rose, and even though she tried to escape from Fred, she agreed to go back with him back to Midland Road.

During the 1970s, Gloucester was made up largely of West Indians which created fun and extra money for Rose and Fred. Rose regularly entertained Caribbean men at the flat and Fred took great pleasure in watching her through the spyhole in the wall. Voyeurism stimulated him far more than the actual sex act. But it was bondage that turned him on more than anything. Fred was never interested in ordinary sex. He was only aroused if it involved bondage, vibrators, defecation, lesbians, threesomes or sadism. Many times, he would take erotic photos of Rose and run them as advertisements in magazines for "swingers".

The children were always only yards away from the bizarre and violent sex that was going on at Midland Road. Heather was often neglected, left in wet and soiled diapers. Anne Marie was almost 8 years old now and Fred started fantasizing about the pleasure the little girl could give him.

Elizabeth Agius, one of Fred and Rose's neighbors and sex partners, said Rose had told her that Anne Marie had lost her virginity when she fell off her bicycle and one of the handlebars had entered her vagina. Were the Wests simply trying to see if their neighbor was interested in paedophilia, or were they telling the story so that they could use it later to cover up the sexual abuse?

In the meantime, in August 1971, desperate to locate Charmaine, Rena visited Fred's father, Walter, in hopes of finding out what happened to her daughter. Fearing Rena would learn the truth, Fred saw no choice but to kill her. It's believed that Fred got Rena drunk at a pub and then strangled her, possibly by inserting a tube down her throat, since a short length of narrow tubing was later found with her remains along with a small plastic boomerang. Both items may have been used to abuse Rena's body in other ways. Fred took her body back to Midland Road where he dismembered it in the same manner as he had done with Anna McFall's, cutting off Rena's fingers and toes. When he was done, he put her remains into garbage bags and buried her in the same general location that he had buried Anna McFall. Since no one reported Rena missing, Fred had gotten away with murder—again.

◆ ◆ ◆

On January 29, 1972, Fred and Rose were married in Gloucester. With a growing family they needed a larger house along with a place to accommodate Rose's prostitution business, so they moved to 25 Cromwell Street and took in young boarders to help pay the rent. The house was spacious with two upstairs floors, a ground floor, and a garage and cellar which would later be soundproofed and used as the West's torture chamber.

It wasn't long before Rose was having sex with the male lodgers, with Fred likely leering through a peephole, and the house became a sexual free-for-all. One of the male lodgers started to bring home a buxom brunette named Lynda Gough, a seamstress and the daughter of a firefighter. When she was 17 years-old, she met Fred and Rose and they became friendly. Fred explained they were in the need a of a nanny to care for the children. The meeting would eventually prove fatal.

In June, Rose gave birth to another daughter, May (later changed to Mae). Now there were four children in the house.

Sometime in the summer during the first year at Cromwell Street, 8-year-old Anne Marie was led to the cellar by her father and stepmother. There she saw Pyrex bowl, clothes, and a vibrator. Rose removed her clothes and Anne Marie started to cry. But no one could hear her outside the soundproof walls. Her hands were bound, and she was gagged.

While Fred forced her legs open and raped her, Rose watched and clearly was having fun. Anne Marie would later go on to say, "She [Rose] was laughing, smirking and saying to me it was for my own good and to stop being silly."

She watched her father remove "strange red-colored matter" from inside her and place it in the Pyrex bowel. Left in excruciating pain after her ordeal, Anne Marie was kept from school for several days and was told by Rose if she spoke to anyone about what happened, she would be beaten.

Sometime later, Rose asked Anne Marie to clean the cellar which doubled as the children's playroom. On the back wall she noticed an unusual long bar bent into U-shaped frame fitted with handles. The sight scared her. When she turned, Rose was behind her, blocking the doorway. Her stepmother ordered her to undress and she was gagged, and then strapped to the frame. Fred came home for lunch and quickly raped his daughter before returning to work. Afterward, Rose abused the girl with a vibrator. Rose commanded the cut and bruised Anne Marie to take a bath in saltwater, saying it was good for her.

In late 1972, Fred and Rose picked up an extremely attractive 17-year-old named Caroline Owens and hired her as a nanny. The Wests found Caroline so beautiful that Fred and Rose competed with each other to seduce her. Caroline, who wanted no part of their sex games, told them that she was leaving, so the couple abducted and raped her. When they were done, Fred made it clear to Caroline what would happen if she didn't do what he wanted.

"I'll keep you in the cellar and let my black friends have you, and when we're finished we'll kill you and bury you under the paving stones of Gloucester."

Terrified, she told her mother who called the police.

A hearing was set in January of 1973 when Fred was 31 and Rose was 19 and pregnant again. Since Fred was able to con the magistrate into believing that Caroline was a willing partner, the couple walked away with a mere fine.

Over time, the Wests had continued their friendship with seamstress Lynda Gough. Eventually, she moved into 25 Cromwell Street to take care of the children, but something went wrong and Lynda was murdered. Fred dismembered her body and buried her in a pit in the garage. He removed her fingers, toes, and kneecaps to keep as trophies.

In August, Rose gave birth to their first son, Stephen.

Excited by their success in getting away with the murder of Lynda Gough and the Caroline Owens rape and abduction charge, the Wests abducted 15-year-old Carol Ann Cooper on November 10, 1973. When they were done with her sexually, they killed her, and Fred dismembered her and buried her remains with the growing list of victims buried at 25 Cromwell Street.

Lucy Partington, a 21-year-old university student vanished on December 27, from a bus stop after visiting a friend. Lucy was tortured for approximately a week much like Carol Ann Cooper and then murdered, dismembered, and buried in the cellar. While Fred was dismembering Lucy, he seriously cut himself and had to go to the hospital for stitches on January 3, 1974. When Lucy's skeleton was discovered, it was missing a number of finger and toe bones, the left kneecap, the right shoulder blade and four ribs. A knife was found with the remains that matched Fred's injury. Lucy, like Carol Ann Cooper, was reported missing, but there was no evidence to tie the two young women to the Wests.

Between Easter in April of 1974 and April of 1975, three women; Therese Siegenthaler, 21, Shirley Hubbard, 15, and Juanita Mott, 18, met the same gruesome fate as Carol Ann Cooper and Lucy Partington. Their abused, tortured and dismembered bodies were buried in the cellar of the Wests' home.

Since bondage was what excited Fred and Rose the most, Shirley Hubbard's head had been encased completely with tape. A plastic tube was inserted into her nose so she could breathe while the Wests tortured and raped her. According to Howard Sounes, Juanita Mott was:

"Gagged with a ligature made from two long, white nylon socks (similar to those worn by Rose), a brassiere and two pairs of tights, one within the other. She was then trussed up with lengths of plastic-covered rope, of the type used for washing line. The rope was used in a complicated way, with loops tied around her arms and thighs, both wrists, both ankles and her skull, horizontally and vertically, backwards and forwards across her body until she could only wriggle like a trapped animal. Then the Wests produced a seven-foot length of rope with a slipknot end forming a noose. This was probably used to suspend Juanita's body from the beams in the cellar." (Sounes, 1995)

Considering there were bodies piling up at 25 Cromwell Street, Fred continued to commit petty thefts and fenced stolen items in order to financially front his numerous home improvement projects. This construction work was necessary to keep his and Rose's horrific hobby hidden below the layers of concrete.

In 1976, Fred and Rosemary lured a young female (designated by the courts as "Miss A") from a home for troubled young girls. At the Wests' home, Miss A was guided into a room where two naked girls were held prisoner. Miss A first witnessed the torture of the two girls and was then raped by Fred and sexually assaulted by Rose. One of the girls that Miss A claimed to see was likely Anne Marie, who was a constant target of the

Wests' sexual sadism. It was bad enough that Fred raped and tortured his own daughter, but he also brought home some of his friends to have sex with her.

In 1977, the upstairs of the Wests' house was remodeled to allow for a number of new lodgers. 18-year-old Shirley Robinson, a former prostitute, was one of them. Because Shirley was bisexual, she developed relationships with both Fred and Rose. She became pregnant with Fred's child and at the time Rose was pregnant with the child of one of her black clients. Even though Fred was thrilled that his wife was carrying a mixed-race child, Rose became very uncomfortable with Shirley carrying Fred's child. Rose believed that the younger woman would try to replace her, so she made it clear—Shirley had to disappear.

months after Rose gave birth in December 1977 to Tara, Shirley Robinson joined the many girls buried at Cromwell Street. Since the cellar was full, she was buried in the rear garden near the back door of the house along with her unborn child. This time, Fred not only dismembered Shirley, he also dismembered her unborn child. *His* unborn child.

In November of 1978, Rose and Fred had their sixth child, a daughter they named Louise. Fred had also impregnated Anne Marie, but the pregnancy was terminated because it occurred in one of her fallopian tubes.

Months after Rose's father died in May 1979,

the Wests murdered a troubled teenager named Alison Chambers after they raped and tortured her. Just like Shirley Robinson, Alison was buried in the rear garden.

The other children were aware of what was going on—that Rose was a prostitute and that Anne Marie was being raped by her father. When Anne Marie finally moved out to live with her boyfriend, Fred focused his sexual advances on Heather and Mae. Heather fought off her father and was beaten for it.

Rose gave birth to Fred's second son, Barry, in June of 1980. Again, in April of 1982, Rosemary Junior was born, who was not Fred's child. Another daughter followed in July 1983, who they named Lucyanna. She was half-black like Rosemary Junior and Tara. With so many children in the house, Rose became progressively irrational, losing her temper and beating the children without any provocation.

In 1986, Heather told one of her girlfriends about her father's sexual advances, and the beatings she received. The girlfriend told her parents, who were friends of the Wests, and Heather's life was suddenly in danger. No one knows exactly what happened in June 1987, or which of the Wests actually strangled Heather, but it was Fred's duty to dispose of the remains. He likely employed a heavy serrated knife used for cutting up frozen meat, and held his dead daughter face down, cutting clear through the back of her neck to decapitate her. He removed parts of her hands, feet, and kneecaps, and possibly yanked out her fingernails. Fred put her remains in black garbage bags to be buried later in the garden. Since her skeleton was discovered with no clothes, Heather was likely sexually abused and/or tortured. Whether the abuse happened before or after she was killed is unclear.

Fred and Rose West's luck was about to run out. One of the extremely young girls that Fred had sexually abused with Rose's assistance told a friend about what happened. After the girlfriend went to the police, the case was assigned to Detective Constable Hazel Savage. Detective Superintendent John Bennett was in charge of the case. Hazel was familiar with Fred from his days with Rena and recalled the stories Rena had told her about Fred's sexual perversions.

The police arrived at 25 Cromwell Street on August 6, 1992 with a warrant to search for pornography and evidence of child abuse. They found plenty! Fred was arrested for sodomy and rape of a minor, and Rose for assisting him. The younger West children were placed into government care.

After, Hazel Savage interviewed family members and friends of the Wests and talked to Anne Marie and learned heard how horribly the girl had been abused. Hazel was not satisfied that Heather had simply disappeared without a trace. She feared the rumor was true—that Heather was buried under the patio...

In contrast, when Fred learned that human bones had been discovered in his yard, he confessed once again to murdering his daughter, but adamantly denied that there were bones belonging to anyone else there. He went on to tell the detectives what had happened.

Fred, who was a compulsive lair, claimed he had argued in the hallway of his house with his headstrong daughter and had slapped her for being cheeky with him. When she wouldn't stop laughing at him, he snatched her by her throat. As Fred recounted his story, he frequently stopped for a cigarette but overall seemed relaxed; as if it was no big deal that he'd killed his own daughter. He claimed he must have held her too hard because Heather suddenly turned blue and stopped breathing. When he tried to revive her, he realized he didn't have the proper training, so he dragged her into the bathtub and ran cold water over her. Afterward, he removed her clothing, lifted her out of the tub, and dried her off. When he put her in the garbage bin to keep her hidden from family member, she didn't fit.

Knowing he had to make her smaller to fit into the bin, he put her back to the tub and strangled her with a pair of tights to make sure she was dead.

"I didn't want to touch her while she was alive. I mean if I'd have started cutting her leg or her throat and she'd have suddenly come alive." He decided to close Heather's eyes before he dismembered her. "If somebody's sat there looking at you, you're not going to use a knife on that person, are you?"

He began with her head and remembered a "horrible noise like scrunching": a sound he found very displeasing. After her head was off, he started working on her legs, twisting her foot until he heard "one almighty crack and the leg come loose, like." Once he had her cut into pieces, she fit perfectly into the garbage bin.

That night while his family was sleeping, he proceeded to bury Heather's body in the garden, where she stayed undetected for seven years. When asked about the missing parts of Heather's skeleton, Fred offered no explanation.

As the police continued their gruesome task between February to June 7, 1994, the corpses of 12 bodies were discovered. five were buried in the cellar at Cromwell Street, three were unearthed underneath the patio of the back garden. Charmaine's skeleton was found at the house on Midland Road. Anna McFall's and Rena West's remains were excavated in two separate fields near Much Marcle.

Rose continued to deny any involvement and was not arrested until April 1994 when she was was charged with ten murders. Fred was charged with eleven.

While awaiting trial, Fred West, prisoner WN-3617, was held in Winson Green Prison in Birmingham in a cell by himself because the prison officials feared he could be a target of violent inmates looking for notoriety.

On January 1, 1995, Fred was in his cell unsupervised. He tore his bed sheets into strips and fashioned them into a ligature which he tied to an air vent directly above his cell door. At approximately 12:55 PM, he was discovered hanging lifeless and was pronounced dead at 1:22 AM. There has been a lot of speculation as to why Fred committed suicide: that he was depressed, his confessions to the police guaranteed a lifetime behind bars, his suicide would help Rose, and his claim that he had killed up to 20 more women that were still undiscovered by the police. Lastly, after the Wests' arrests, Rose became distant from her husband—the love of his life, his soul mate had abandoned him and left him devastated.

On October 3, 1995, Rose West's trial began at Winchester Court and ended on November 20 after she took the stand in her own defence and portrayed herself as a defiant aggressor who treated her children atrociously. She was found guilty on all 10 counts and was sentenced to 25 years in prison. However, in 1997 Home Secretary Jack Straw subjected Rose to a whole life tariff. This was only the second case in modern times, that a British woman was condemned to die in prison.

The other was child killer Myra Hindley.

On November 18, 1999, Anne Marie (now Anne Marie Davies), the daughter of Fred West was rescued from a river in Gloucester after someone reported seeing a person fall from a nearby bridge. Following the rescue, she was taken to Gloucestershire Royal Hospital and later discharged. On a previous occasion, she had attempted to kill herself by taking an overdose of pills during her stepmother's trial but survived after being rushed to a nearby hospital to have her stomach pumped.

As for Rose West, on September 30, 2001, she announced that she would not appeal her conviction and continues to maintain her innocence. Today, she is held at HMP Low Newton in Durham. The 60-year-old has her own room complete with a TV, radio, CD player and private bathroom. She enjoys living behind bars at the top-security prison where she listens to *The Archers* on Radio 4, plays Monopoly, enjoys embroidery, cooking, and shopping from catalogues.

In a statement released to the *Mail*, West spoke for the first time since her conviction and said, "Despite everything, I should like at some stage to apologize to Anne Marie. Anne Marie is part of my family and I would love to be reconciled to her and have contact with her." West also stated that "she had come to understand herself, and her relationships with others, for the first time in her life".

The macabre dissected trophies that Fred West kept, the fingers, toes, kneecaps and other body parts have never been found.

The three-storey house at 25 Cromwell Street, known to many as the "house of horrors", along with the adjoining property, was demolished in 1996, but the physical removal of the brick structure would not erase the depraved and hideous crimes that the Wests committed together—nor would they ever be forgotten.

Sources

Sounes, Howard (1995). Fred and Rose: The Full Story of Fred and Rose West and the Gloucester House of Horrors. Warner Books (London).

Wilson, Colin (2003). The Corpse Garden: The Crimes of Fred and Rose West. Pan Books

Woodrow, Jane Carter. Rose West: The Making of a Monster. Hodder & Stoughton

Crime Library: Fred and Rose West. Marilyn Bardsley. http://www.crimelibrary.com/serial_killers/weird/west/index_1.html

Daily Mail. Stephen Wright. Avon, Monopoly and The Archers: Why Rose West loves life in jail so much she wants to die there. http://www.dailymail.co.uk/news/article-2565316/Avon-Monopoly-The-Archers-Why-Rose-West-loves-life-jail.html

CHAPTER SIX

Joesph Kallinger

Joseph Michael Kallinger was born at the Northern Liberties Hospital in Philadelphia on December 11, 1936, to Judith Renner an unwed mother who gave him up for adoption soon after his birth.

Two months before his second birthday, Joseph was adopted by Catholic Austrian immigrants, Stephen and Anna Kallinger. But growing up with his new adoptive parents was far from the loving and nurturing relationship most young children experience. Instead, Joseph's upbringing was unloving, cruel and sadistic due to his mother, a strict disciplinarian, and his father an abusive German immigrant.

Anytime he got out of line his parents would whip him with cat-o'-nine-tails, hit him with a hammer, made him keel on jagged rocks and sandpaper, locked him closets, burned with him irons, forced him to eat excrement, starved him, and would make continuous threats of castration to ensure he did as he was told.

In the fall of 1943, at age six, Joseph suffered a hernia due to being kicked in the groin by a girl. Even though he claimed he didn't do anything to deserve the kick, his parents punished him anyway. After his hernia was repaired his parents told him that doctors had done the surgery to keep his "bird" (Bird was the word used in the Kallinger house for penis.) small.

'He fixed your hernia ... but he also fixed ... your little bird.'

In the Kallinger home, 'bird' was the euphemism for penis.

'What's wrong with my little bird?' Joe asked.

'An evil spirit ... a demon makes your bird get hard and stick out so you do bad things with it. Then your soul goes to the Devil when you die ... but
you won't have no demon, because your bird will always be small, small, small!'

— Christiane Olivier, Jocasta's Children: The Imprint of the Mother Routledge, London, and NY, 1989

By the age of seven, the young boy had lived a lonely existence spending each day after school and Saturdays doing chores and repairing shoes in his father's shop.

Two years later Joseph was threatened with a

knife by older neighborhood boys while one of them performed oral sex on him. Later in life, Kallinger claimed the incident traumatized him immensely, so much so, that he began to associate sex with violence and would masturbate with a knife in his hand.

By thirteen he was masturbating on a regular basis using naked pictures of men and women but over time he found that he needed to stab the photographs to become aroused. Then he began to hear voices.

After returning from camp, voices told him to cut someone, so he boarded a city bus with a knife. When he saw a boy exit the bus, he followed him into the woods where he ordered the boy at knife point to take off his pants then Joseph would run away leaving the boy unharmed. Kallinger did these three more times over the next few months. The final time he re-enacted what had been done to him when he was nine by putting the boy's penis in his mouth and bite it while holding him at knife point.

In the spring of 1950, Kallinger met a girl named, Hilda, and a relationship bloomed. He decided to move out of the house so he could see her since his parents did not approve and demanded that he stop seeing her.

By 1951 he was hearing voices again. This time God gave him a different mission—to heal and save people through his feet. Between 1951 and 1972, Kallinger conducted over 40,000 experiments due to his new order from God.

Still working in his father's shoe shop, Kallinger dropped out of school at the age of seventeen and married Hilda. They have two children together however their marriage is far from perfect. Fed up with Joseph's abuse, Hilda left him for another man. Three years later they divorced.

The following year he was hospitalized for headaches, but his real problem would be revealed as an anxiety disorder.

He married for the second time in April 1958 and had five children with his wife, Beth. Shortly after they wed, their relationship turned abusive. Tempers flared almost on a daily basis and he inflicted the same type of punishments on his children that he had suffered from his adoptive parents.

His mental issues also continued to plague him. After a failed suicide attempt in 1959, he was admitted to a state hospital and released after a brief stay.

It would be fourteen years later when Joseph Kallinger would be arrested for abuse.

On January 30, 1972, three of the Kallinger children, Mary Jo, Joe Jr and Michael, walked into the police station and accused their father of burning and beating them. The policewoman who examined them found that Mary Jo's buttocks were covered with crisscross type lacerations and she had a recent three-inch burn on her inner thigh. Joe Jr (Joey) had bruises on his forehead, a black eye, and bruising on both of his hands. Both Kallinger and his wife denied the abuse accusations saying children had run away.

Ten-year-old Michael said his father had beaten him with leather soles taken from the shoe shop, with belts, and using the handle of a hammer.

Thirty-six-year-old Joseph Kallinger was arrested that night. Unable to raise $75,000 bail, Kallinger remained in prison for seven months and underwent court-ordered psychiatric examinations. While he was incarcerated, he scored 82 on an IQ test and was diagnosed with paranoid schizophrenia. Despite having a major mental illness, his bail was reduced to $5,000.

Deemed competent to stand trial, Kallinger was found guilty of child abuse. He was sentenced to four years of probation with mandatory psychiatric treatment and a provision that 12-year-old Mary Jo be removed from the family home. State psychiatrists also recommended that he be supervised with his family.

Six months later, Mary Jo and Joe Jr recanted their statements and their father petitioned the court in February 1974 for a retrial. At the retrial hearing, Kallinger produced evidence, a letter dated December 11, 1973, from Mary Jo in which she stated she had made up the story to the police about her father burning her because "it was just something I said to make them scare you into letting me have some fun."

Other evidence at the hearing included two diaries belonging to Joey marked throughout with "I hate my dad." In one of his notebooks he wrote, "Maybe I can get my brother and sister to put him in jail...be easy to say dad did it. I have the markings."

It was discovered that Joey's black eye was received during a street fight; his bruised hands caused by boys "stepping on him". He was declared 'incorrigible' and was committed to serving four months at the Eastern State School and Hospital, a reform school and psychiatric facility. Joey Jr returned home on May 15.

In a fluster of well-targeted publicity, Joseph Kallinger claimed he had forgiven his children for the false abuse allegations. "Who said kids had to be perfect," he said to the media.

Throughout 1974, Joseph Kallinger claimed he was hallucinating constantly and holding regular conversations with a disembodied head named, Charlie. He also said he was receiving personal orders from God.

❖ ❖ ❖

In early June Kallinger told his 13-year-old son, Michael, about his orders from God to murder young boys and sever their genitals. He asked for his son's help and Michael agreed. The victim—a neighborhood boy, ten-year-old Jose Collazo who according to Kallinger was picked at random in a plan to begin his "world massacre".

Joseph Kallinger said they took Jose to an abandon rug factory in Kensington where they suffocated the boy, cut off his penis, and shoved a pair of shears into his rectum. He also claimed he kept the dismembered penis. The boy's body was found on July 7.

A month later he took out a hefty life insurance policy on his son Joey and his younger son, James. On July 28, Kallinger reported Joey Jr missing stating the teenager had run away from home.

On August 8, Joey's body was discovered in a pool of water at a building demolition site in the 900 block of Market Street.

"Joey was an exploring-type boy," Kallinger said after identifying the body by photographs and clothing. "I guess he was on one of his adventures".

The insurance company suspected foul play and refused to pay out the insurance claim.

This wasn't the first time Kallinger had tried to make some easy money. About a decade earlier he had an insurance policy on a building which ended up damaged by fire and collected $15,000. A week later there was a second fire and then a third where the insurance company paid on the claims. When the fourth fire broke out in a vacant building Kallinger was charged with arson but the charges were later dropped due to the lack of evidence.

As far as Joey's death was concerned, the cause of death could not be determined at the time. It wasn't until Kallinger later admitted to Flora Rheta Schreiber, author of *Sybil,* and *The Shoemaker* (the 1983 book written by Schreiber and co-authored by Joseph Kallinger) that he had drowned his son by chaining a ladder to him in the pool.

During the first week of October, Kallinger took his 13-year-old son, Michael, to Frankford Hospital with a head injury. He stated the boy had "slipped and fell". Michael was treated and sent home. When his son began vomiting Kallinger took him to St. Christopher's Hospital for Children where he was treated again and released. The following day, Michael was spotted by a security guard wandering around the lobby at Cooper Hospital in Camden. He was disoriented and unable to talk but was able to write down his name. The police called his father and Michael was taken home.

It was clear that Joseph Kallinger had not forgiven his children for their false accusations of abuse, especially Joey Jr, who paid with his life. And things were about to get worse as Kallinger's campaign of "global massacre" was about to kick into high gear. To begin…he would need to finance the massacre.

November 22, 1974

On a frigid Friday afternoon in the sleepy community of Lindenwold, New Jersey, a 21-year-old mother was busy with her two young children when a boy knocked at the door. When she answered the door, the teenager asked if she wanted to buy some cufflinks and tie clips. Little did she know that another house, a mile and a half away had been burglarized earlier in the afternoon by a man and a boy.

The woman politely told the boy she didn't want any. The boy thanked her and then left. Twenty minutes later there was another knock at the door. This time it was a man dressed in a dark suit, tie, and overcoat. He appeared to be about 45 years old. Thinking he might be the boy's father or perhaps even a detective looking for the boy, the woman opened the screen door. The man shoved his way into the house and knocked her to the floor. After pulling out a knife from a brown paper bag, he held the knife against her throat and said, "Don't scream or make a sound, or I'll cut you."

Fearing for the safety of her children, the woman obeyed. Then a second intruder entered the house. She couldn't see him but she recognized his voice. It was the boy who was at the front door earlier.

After the man gagged her with a pair of her husband's jockey shorts and bound her ankles with rawhide laces he'd brought with him in the paper bag, he ordered the woman to do what was described as a "perverted sex act" on him while her children slept in their bedrooms.

Afterward, the man and boy rummaged through her home loading jewelry and small appliances into suitcases they had taken from the attic. Before leaving, the man rifled through her wallet and removed one hundred dollars. They left the house at approximately 4:40 p.m., almost two hours after they'd arrived, and then vanished.

December 3, 1974

At approximately 11 a.m., north of Harrisburg, Pennsylvania, at 3509 Green Street, Helen Bogin, a blonde middle-aged woman left her white framed house with red shutters and went to run some errands. When she returned a half hour later to prepare for her afternoon bridge luncheon with neighbors, she unlocked her front door and a large hand snatched her by the neck and yanked her inside.

A male voice from behind her said if she screamed, she would be killed. A teenage boy stood quietly a few feet away and watched.

The man put a knife to her throat and told her they were going upstairs to the bedroom. On the way, he bound her hands with rawhide laces.

When she said, "Why don't you get a job instead of what you're doing!", the man reached around her shoulder and pierced her blouse with the knife.

She didn't realize until afterward that she was covered in blood, and never felt the knife cutting her skin.

While the boy continued to watch, the man ripped the sheets and mattress off the bed. He proceeded to tell Helen to lay face down on the springs. He undid the laces and instructed her to get undressed. Once she was naked, he bound her wrists again and her ankles. He said if she didn't make a fuss, he wouldn't kill her.

The front doorbell suddenly rang sending the boy and man running quietly down the stairs.

Ethal Cohen had arrived for lunch and bridge.

The man swung the door open, grabbed Ethal, and threw her on the floor in the foyer. When she fell, she "caught a glimpse of a middle-aged man and a teenaged boy wearing a ski cap".

In a second bedroom, Ethal was forced to remove her clothing and lay face down on the bed. The man tied her hands behind her, bound her feet and shoved a pillowcase over her head.

Then the doorbell rang again.

Thelma Sudin arrived at approximately 12:30 p.m. Within minutes she was lying on the foyer floor with the barrel of a gun pressed to her face.

After warning her to cooperate, he took her upstairs and made her get undressed in the hallway. Without any rawhide laces left, the man cut the electric cord off an appliance and bound her hands and feet. Before putting a pillowcase over her head, he took a 2 1/2 carat diamond engagement ring off her finger and removed a bracelet. He then shoved her in a closet and shut the door.

Just when the man was telling the boy to grab all the loot, the doorbell rang again.

Annapearl Frankston was the last guest to arrive at 12:45.

The door flew open and Frankston found herself pulled inside and flat on the floor within seconds. The man seized her by the neck and shoved a gun in her face to stop her from screaming so loudly.

He removed her clothes, snatched her wedding and engagement rings and stole her purse. Afterward, he forced her into the bathroom and down onto the floor.

With all the women were secure and out of the way, the man and boy quickly collected the jewelry, cash and small appliances worth an estimated $20,000 and made their escape by bus back into Harrisburg.

December 10, 1974

Late in the afternoon in the upper-class community of Homeland, located in north Baltimore, Pamela Jaske, an attractive 28-year-old returned home to her two-story white frame house with her four-month-old daughter following a trip to the post office around the corner.

After putting the baby down for a nap on the second floor, she heard a loud rap on her front door. Then she heard the door open followed by footsteps thundering up the stairs.

A boy held a knife in his hand and the man had a gun. The man said if she screamed her would kill her baby. Fearing for her child, Jaske told the man she would be quiet. Moments later she was in her bedroom and told to remove her clothes. Her hands and ankles were handcuffed, and tape was wound around her eyes and head. Then the man asked her where she kept her money and valuables. After he instructed the boy to gather the valuables in a blue tote bag, they'd brought with them, the boy left the room.

With the gun pointed at Pamela's Jaske's head, the man instructed her to perform oral sex on him. When he was done, he moved her into the bathroom and bound her with a cord from a vacuum cleaner to the drainpipe underneath the sink and then stuffed a sock in her mouth.

When there was a knock at the front door the man froze. Luckily, the caller didn't knock again.

Minutes later, the two intruders ran out the front door with thousands of dollars worth of jewelry and photographic equipment. It's believed they boarded a Northbound M.T.A bus, the "11 Dunkirk".

January 6, 1975

At 9:10 a.m., Mary Rudolph, 39, was looking out the bay window of her split-level home at 92 Harrison Street in Dumont, New Jersey when she spotted a man and boy who she'd seen earlier wandering throughout the neighborhood. Before calling the police, she slipped to the bathroom and when she emerged, she was startled by two figures behind a Plexiglass room divider.

Before she knew it, the man jumped out and forced a piece of white tape over her eyes. He asked if she had a coin collection. She told him she didn't but there was some money on the dresser upstairs in the bedroom. She said she would show him if he didn't harm her child.

Mary Rudolph's two-and-a-half-year-old son was sitting on the living room floor watching TV and eating breakfast. The man grabbed the child from the floor and followed Mary up to the second storey of the house where he deposited the child in a small bedroom and closed the door.

In the master bedroom, he stripped the mattress off the bed and ordered Mary to undress. Using the electrical cords, he cut from two lamps in the room, he tied her feet and hands to four coil springs.

While the boy ransacked the main floor, the man removed $500 cash from the dresser and told

Mary not to tell the kid that he had the money. He proceeded to tell her if she didn't cooperate by performing fellatio on him, he would harm the child. With no choice, she did what she was told and when he was done, he said he was sending the boy up and she needed to do whatever he wanted her to do. He yelled for the boy to come up and then left the room.

The boy had removed his clothes preparing himself to rape Mary, however, within moments he became frustrated and abandoned the idea. The intruders then loaded suitcases full of valuables including jewelry, an eight-track stereo, and small appliances.

By the time, Mary Rudolph's daughter had returned home from school the man and adolescent boy were long gone more than likely taking the No. 86 bus from Chestnut Bend to the Port Authority terminal under the George Washington Bridge.

January 8, 1975

Leonia, New Jersey, is located eight miles southeast of Dumont and in the mid-seventies had a population of approximately 9,300 residents.

Edwina Wiseman, 26, lived at 124 Glenwood Avenue. Known as "Dee Dee" to her friends, she had just finished giving her four-year-old son, Robert, lunch and was vacuuming while her grandmother, Blanche Smith rested upstairs. When the doorbell rang, Edwina, shut off the vacuum and went to the door.

Standing on the front porch was a dark-haired man dressed in a suit and coat. He introduced himself as a salesman with John Hancock Insurance. After asking if he could come in to discuss his business Dee Dee told him she wasn't interested in insurance.

The man barreled into her and thrust her backward forcing the front door open. Once inside, she realized he had a gun in one hand and a knife in the other. Behind him was a slender teenage boy wearing an olive-green ski parka and ski hat with a pompom.

The man aimed the gun at her and ordered her to take off her clothes. She obeyed, then he bound her hands and feet, taped her mouth and took her and her four-year-old son upstairs. In the bedroom, the man told the small child to remove all his clothing. When the child was naked the man made it clear that they were only in the house to take some things and as long as no one screamed no harm would come them. With Edwina's 90-year-old grandmother sitting in another bedroom, unaware of what was going on, the man and teenager rifled through the house, collecting jewelry, cash, and traveler's checks.

Then the doorbell rang.

The man answered the door to find a pretty 21-year-old woman with brown hair (Randi

Romaine). Once the woman was stripped naked and bound, the man moved her to a bedroom upstairs. Four others walked into the house, Dewitt Romaine (Randi's mother), Retta (Randi's twin sister), and her boyfriend, Jeffery Welby. They were quickly met by the armed intruders then tied up with cord cut from the blinds.

Once again, the doorbell rang.

This time it was a cute brunette, a 21-year-old nurse who worked at Hackensack Hospital and lived two blocks away. Her name was Maria Fasching.

Little did Maria know that her fate would be sealed when she was met at the door by a man with a gun and a teenager holding a knife.

Her mouth and eyes were taped. As the man secured her hands behind her back using a piece of cord from the blinds, Maria wriggled and fought against the restraints. The man became angry and said he would kill her if she didn't do exactly as he ordered.

With the others battened down and threatened to remain quiet, in the basement, the man instructed Maria to undress. When she refused, he held a knife to her.

"But you said you weren't going to hurt us," she cried.

He pressed his body against hers and ordered her to perform oral sex on him.

Again, Maria refused.

Infuriated by her defiance, he slashed the

young woman's neck three times.

"Oh, my God, stop it, stop it!" Maria screamed.

He plunged the knife into her back, and then stabbed her in the left breast. The knife pierced her heart and within minutes, Maria Fasching bled out.

After hearing Maria's blood-curdling screams coming from the lower level of the house, Edwina was able to get herself free and to the front yard. "Help! Help! There are two armed men in my basement. My family is in the house. Oh, my God. Oh, my God."

A neighbor quickly called the police.

The teenage boy spotted Edwina in the yard. The man tore up the stairs, grabbed his accomplice, and together they fled out the back door leaving the loot; small appliances and jewelry.

Once the boy and man were a safe distance from the house, the man tried to scrub Maria Fasching's blood from his shirt in a puddle in Sylvan Park. When he looked up, he noticed two women watching him. He panicked and bolted with the boy in tow leaving the shirt behind.

The duo then boarded a bus heading south down Grand Avenue out of Leonia to New York. According to the bus driver, the man was shirtless—the teenage boy was wearing a ski hat.

During their 18-month three state burglary escapades, Joseph Kallinger and his son Michael stole $600,000 in jewelry and cash between 1973 and 1975.

❖ ❖ ❖

As the police took the victim's statements, fingerprints were collected from the Romaine house, but authorities were unable to identify who they belonged to.

Not far from the Glenwood Avenue crime scene physical evidence was discovered after a lead from Eva Rumi, who was walking her dog in Sylvan park. When the police checked out the lead, they located a white dress shirt with a blue and gray geometrical pattern woven throughout the fabric near a puddle next to a swing set. The shirt was covered with mud and what appeared to be blood, so investigators focused on the shirt.

The laundry mark on the collar was cleaned and revealed the name 'KALINGER'. The shirt was made for Berg Brothers, a store located on North Front Street in the Kensington area of Philadelphia. When the clerk at the store couldn't remember selling the shirt to the man who the victims had described, investigators decided to check out the various laundry services in the area.

Seven days later, two Bergen County detectives walked into Bright Sun Cleaners on North Front Street. The owner immediately recognized the shirt and said the piece of clothing belonged to Joseph Kallinger, a shoemaker who owned a repair shop at Sterner and Front Streets. He also told them that Kallinger lived above the shoe shop. When asked the why the name on the collar wasn't spelled correctly, the owner explained that the machine used to make the imprint was only able to handle printing eight letters. The second 'L' had to be dropped.

When police ran the correct spelling, they were elated when they got a hit. They learned Kallinger had a previous arrest for child abuse in 1972 and his fingerprints were on file with the Philadelphia police. With the fingerprints lifted from the December 3 burglary at Helen Bogin's residence in Harrisburg, police compared them to the prints belonging to Kallinger. They were a match.

On Friday, January 17 at 9:30 p.m., Joseph Kallinger was arrested along with his two sons, Michael, 13 and James, 11, for burglary, kidnapping, and robbery. Kallinger was held on $100,000 bond. James was released after police discovered that Michael was the accomplice.

Meanwhile, the authorities in Camden County (Lindenwold) and Baltimore simultaneously issued warrants for Joseph and Michael Kallinger for the crimes committed on November 22 and December 10. The pair stood in a line-up for the victims and witnesses from the crimes in Lindenwold, Harrisburg, Baltimore, and Leonia. In addition, two housewives from Lindenworld identified over fifty items that were stolen from their homes. The items were found at Kallinger's home in Kensington.

Joseph Kallinger was imprisoned at the state correctional institution in Huntington where he sat preparing his defense. In August 1975, he plead insanity, but psychiatric evaluations were conducted, and it was determined that he understood right from wrong and was deemed competent to stand trial.

After his first trial was declared a mistrial during jury selection his second trial began in September. Kallinger brought a Bible and *The Life of Christ* with him which he read during the jury selection paying little attention to what was going on unless his lawyer asked him a question. Charged with four counts of robbery, 4 counts of false imprisonment and one count of burglary, Kallinger testified he couldn't remember things and that God communicated with him and told him what to do. He also said he was the son of God and had existed as a butterfly.

His attorneys claimed Kallinger suffered from "toxic derangement" caused from inhaling the chemicals he used in his shoe repair shop.

It took the Bergen County jury less than an hour to find Joseph Kallinger guilty. The judge told Kallinger that he was an evil man. Not only had treated his victims badly but had even threatened one of them that he would return to "get" her. He also exposed his own child to his crimes, and "to corrupt your own son is vile and depraved." He viewed the defendant as violent and dangerous. Kallinger was sentenced to not less than 30 and not more than 80 years.

Michael, then 13, plead guilty to two counts of armed robbery in exchange for dropping the murder charge. He was placed on probation because it was believed he was manipulated and tortured by his father. Michael changed his name and his whereabouts are unknown.

While Joseph Kallinger waited in jail for his trial in Hackensack, New Jersey to begin in the stabbing death of Maria Fasching he began to act out trying to draw attention to his mental illness. He threw excrement at guards, clogged his toilet to stop "Charlie" from getting him, and mixed his own urine with plum juice and orange juice to pass it off as evidence that he was ill. But his charades didn't work. It was determined by the consulting psychiatrist that Kallinger was faking probably realizing he would never be released from prison.

During the trial in September 1976, his courtroom behavior was strange, off-the-wall, and even appeared psychotic-like. He kicked his feet, chirped, and shouted until he was removed from the courtroom. Most onlookers believed he was putting on a show for the jury.

"As he sat at the defense table, the Philadelphia cobbler's head bobbed and jerked, then swung in clockwise arcs, continually in motion."

Joseph Kallinger bobbing his head during the

trial. Psychiatrist Larry J. McClure testified that Kallinger was feigning insanity to receive a lighter sentence.

Throughout his trial, Kallinger struggled with courtroom officials on several occasions. The defense strategy was to plead insanity, but Kallinger was deemed to be sane and fit to stand trial.

The jury didn't buy into his insanity performance. Joseph Baeli, one of the jurors said. "I think he's crazy, but he's not insane...It was just an act."

On October 13, 1976, at the age of 40, Kallinger was found guilty and sentenced to life in prison. He was also convicted of contributing to the delinquency of his son. He stood emotionless when the verdicts were read.

While behind bars his behavior turned violent. Between March and April of 1977, Kallinger set himself on fire, assaulted another inmate and set his cell block on fire and tried to suffocate himself with plastic. Kallinger was transferred to a hospital in Waymart, Pennsylvania for the criminally insane where tried to kill another prisoner.

In March 1978, in an unprovoked attack, he slashed another inmate's throat. The victim survived.

He was also serving a 42-to-51-year term for the November 22, 1974 robbery and attempted rape in Lindenwold, N.J.

While serving his sentences, he collaborated with New York writer Flora Rheta Schreiber on a book, *The Shoemaker*, in which he admitted to murdering his older son, Joseph Jr., Jose Collazo, and Maria Fasching.

He was convicted on Jan. 31, 1984, for the three murders and sentenced to two life terms to be served consecutively after the robbery sentences.

During television interviews in 1988, Kallinger expressed his continuing desire to slaughter every person on earth and commit suicide so he could become God.

He was readmitted to Farview State Hospital for the criminally insane in Wayne County on May 17, 1990, from the State Correctional Institution at Huntingdon. On June 22, after claiming he saw Christ in a toilet bowl telling him to join him, he refused to eat or drink, and said he wanted to "meet his maker." He also refused treatment for a foot abscess although eventually agreed to be transferred to Wayne Memorial Hospital in Wayne County, Pennsylvania, in order to have intravenous fluids and antibiotics administered. However, he continued to refusal any nutrition or other medical treatment.

On July 3, 1990, The Commonwealth of Pennsylvania, Department of Public Welfare, (Department), Farview State Hospital, filed a Request for Special Emergency Relief asking the Court for a Declaratory Judgment authorizing the involuntary administration of necessary nutrition, hydration, and medical care.

It was ordered on August 14, 1990, that the Commonwealth of Pennsylvania, Department of Public Welfare, Farview State Hospital, must provide appropriate nutrition through a gastric tube and appropriate medical care to Joseph Kallinger as long as he continued to refuse either.

Joseph Kallinger's commitment to Farview State Hospital was extended indefinitely until such time that the medical and psychiatric staff determined such feeding could be carried out at an appropriate State Correctional Institution.

His self-destructive behavior continued. In September 1990, a routine X-ray at Farview revealed an assortment of metal objects inside his digestive system. According to prison officials, he swallowed paper clips, staples, and his glasses. He also tied rubber bands around his wrists in hopes of cutting off his blood circulation.

According to Jeffrey Wander, his attorney, Kallinger had been swallowing various objects in an attempt to kill himself. Wander also said his client claimed to have had a vision of the Holy Spirit in his toilet bowl, and that "the Lord told him it was time to come home." He was transferred to Cresson prison in December 1990.

Fearing Kallinger would kill himself, he wasn't allowed to wear a prison jumpsuit inside his heated cell; only boxer shorts. When he tried to swallow a spoon, his eating utensils were confiscated, and he was forced fed himself with his hands.

He would spend the next 5 years in solitary confinement on suicide watch.

Joseph Kallinger died at 3 a.m. on May 26, 1996, in the prison infirmary, where he had been taken after a doctor noticed seizure-like symptoms. According to prison officials, he choked on his own vomit. An autopsy revealed the cause of death as cardio-respiratory arrest.

A prison spokesman stated that Kallinger's body was claimed by a son from Philadelphia. It's unclear as to which of his three surviving sons the official was referring to.

"The world is just a little better place now that he's dead,"' said Valerie Collins, Maria Fasching's sister. "But we as a family suffer to this day. We will never stop suffering."

In *The Shoemaker*, Schreiber portrayed Kallinger as a tortured killer driven by the psychotic belief that God had ordered him to slaughter all of mankind. According to the book, he implicated his son, Michael, in all of the crimes. "Michael was to be Joe's commander-in-chief," Schreiber said. "And then Joe would kill Michael and then himself in the end, and through his death, he would become God. This was the road to his own godhood."

Kallinger told reporters by phone in 1990 that

his son Michael hated Joey Jr "because Joey was a homosexual." Then he went on to describe how they had killed him.

"We brought heavy chains with us and we went to a sub-basement and we found a ladder," he told reporters. "We told Joey to step up on one rung and we spread-eagled him, spread his legs and chained them, and spread his hands and chained them. Michael and myself pushed the ladder into some water. He was submerged in water for approximately five minutes and I had a change of heart and I pulled Joey out and unchained him. I felt his pulse and there was no pulse. He was very cold. We left."

According to Elliot Leyton, author of *Hunting Humans: The Rise Of The Modern Multiple Murderer,* "Only a few (such as Joseph Kallinger, and California's Herbert Mullins, who murdered to "stop earthquakes") detach themselves so much from conventional reality that they construct their own universes, thereby entering that state the psychiatrists call madness."

But was Joseph Kallinger insane or had he put on the performance of a lifetime determined to manipulate and control his situation? Was he psychotic? The professionals couldn't agree.

During an interview with Geraldo Rivera, Kallinger was asked why he killed his own son.

"He was a sacrifice. I was to kill three million people on the planet earth, and he was a sacrifice to see if I could murder and move on my own. At the end of murdering all the people on earth I was going to kill my own family and then take my own life and then become God."

    This from a killer who had successfully argued before a judge to be allowed to defend himself in his fourth trial, and who had also filed a federal civil rights suit against Farview State Hospital in 1988 claiming officials had denied him psychiatric treatment. Also, his recollection of the crimes was unusually detailed and coherent for a man who swore he was out of touch with reality, couldn't remember, and wanted to massacre all of mankind.

Sources

Elliott Leyton. *Hunting Humans: The Rise Of The Modern Multiple Murderer*. 2011. McClelland & Stewart Ronald M. Holmes, Stephen T. Holmes. *Serial Murder*. 2009. Sage Publications

Flora Rheta Schreiber. *The Shoemaker: The Anatomy of a Psychotic. 1983.* Simon & Schuster

Patricia A. Martinelli. *True Crime, New Jersey: The State's Most Notorious Criminal Cases.* August 2007. Stackpole Books.

Thomas Plate. *New York* Magazine. *"No Safety in Suburbia: Anatomy of Seven Weeks of Terror"*. March 3, 1975.

Michael Newton. *The Encyclopedia of Serial Killers: A Study of the Chilling Criminal Phenomenon from the Angels of Death to the Zodiac Killer.* 2006. Checkmark Books.

Dominic Sama. *"Joseph Kallinger, Shoemaker Jailed For 3 Infamous Killings".* May 9, 1996. http://articles.philly.com/1996-05-09/news/25625919_1_murder-charge-robbery-sentences-life-terms

Carol Towarnicky. *"The Shoe Drops Source Of Evil No More Serial Killer Joe Kallinger, The `Kensington Cobbler,' Dies At 59 In State Prison".* May 9, 1996.

http://articles.philly.com/1996-05-09/news/25626579_1_state-prison-prison-officials-consecutive-life-terms

COMMONWEALTH PENNSYLVANIA v. JOSEPH KALLINGER (08/14/90)

https://www.prisonlegalnews.org/news/2007/may/15/mentally-ill-pa-prisoner-forced-to-accept-medical-treatment-to-prevent-death/

Digplanet. Joesph Kallinger.___http://www.digplanet.com/wiki/Joseph_Kallinger#References

Greenlief, Christopher; Amanda Hall and Jenna Hafey. "Joseph Kallinger: 'The Shoemaker". Retrieved 2 May 2012.

CHAPTER SEVEN

Cody Legebokoff

On a frigid Saturday night, a Royal Canadian Mounted Police officer from Fort St. James, British Columbia, and another officer from Vanderhoof met on a dark and barren stretch of Highway 27, to exchange case notes since they jointly patrolled the area.

At 9:45 p.m., the officer from Fort St. James eyed a suspicious black half-ton pickup truck speeding out from an unused logging road, a popular area for wildlife poachers. When the Mounties stopped the truck and questioned the driver, neither officer was satisfied with the young man's answers after finding blood on him, his truck, and a backpack in the shape of a monkey. The man claimed he had poached a deer. The Mounties immediately contacted a conservation officer to investigate whether the driver had been illegally hunting.

After the conservation officer arrived, he

retraced the pickup truck's tire tracks along the backwoods trail a half-kilometer up the road. Expecting to find a freshly killed deer or elk, he discovered the lifeless body of a teenage girl near a gavel pit off of Highway 27 between Vanderhoof and Fort St. James. The body had pants on, rolled down around the ankles with the underwear rolled down within the pants.

Investigators from the North District Major Crime Unit and Vanderhoof RCMP cordoned off the area until a thorough scene examination was completed. To preserve any possible evidence at the site, a no-fly restriction of 2000 feet was implemented for a 2-mile radius around the scene. RCMP spokesman Cpl. Dan Moskaluk with the North District Major Crimes Unit said, "The state of the young girl indicated that she had been murdered just hours before the man's arrest."

On Nov. 27, 2010, the RCMP charged 19-year-old Cody Alan Legebokoff of Prince George with first-degree murder in the death of 15-year-old, Loren Donn Leslie, a legally blind 10th grader originally from the Fraser Lake area.

The next day, Legebokoff gave the first of five interviews, changing his story over and over, alleging first that he stumbled across a body, panicked and took off. In a later interview, he admitted he knew Leslie, claiming she had tried to kill herself, so he hit her with a pipe wrench to put her out of her misery. Const. Greg Yanicki told Legebokoff it appeared suspicious seeing someone running away from where Leslie's body was found. Legebokoff stated he got scared. When questioned about the blood found on him, Legebokoff said he touched Leslie and had gotten some blood on his shoes.

Loren Donn Leslie was completely blind in one eye and had only 50% vision in the other. She also had problems with depth perception, but her vision issues weren't something that slowed her down according to her parents. She was a student at Nechako Valley Secondary School in Vanderhoof, a small rural lumber and agricultural community along the Stuart Lake Highway, a spur road to Highway 16 known as the Highway of Tears, which links Prince Rupert to Prince George where 18 girls or women, mostly of aboriginal descent went missing or were killed along the 800 km section since 1969. The notorious stretch of road has been subject to E-PANA, the police task force set up to investigate what happened to the women. (Pana is the Inuit God who looks after souls in the underworld until reincarnation.)

After a postmortem forensic examination was performed at the Kamloops Royal Inlands Hospital, Loren's remains were sent to a forensic expert in Pennsylvania. Police remained tight-lipped as to what they were looking for and were unable to provide details as to the nature of the examination but stated it was "certainly necessary and an important step to take".

According to her family and friends, Loren

was a kind and generous happy-go-lucky girl that occasionally experienced bouts of depression and at times made impulsive decisions, such as hitchhiking on the highway near her home. She was last seen by her family in Fort St. James on Saturday afternoon after she said she was going to have coffee with a friend. She never returned.

Cpl. Dan Moskaluk declined to say whether Loren Donn Leslie knew the suspect, nor would he reveal any details as to how the teenager was killed or the injuries she sustained. No autopsy findings were released at the time. It was later revealed that she had died from a combination of blood loss and a brain injury that resulted from a series of massive blows to the head causing extensive blunt force trauma and two stab wounds to her neck.

One Of Canada's Youngest Serial Killers

Born on January 1, 1990, blonde-haired and baby-faced, standing 6-foot-2 and weighing 220 pounds, Cody Legebokoff was described as a popular and well-adjusted young man who came from a prosperous and respected family. His parents were married at the age of 19 and he described his childhood as normal with loving parents. He has an older brother and older sister. During his secondary school years, he competed in downhill skiing and snowboarding in northern British Columbia's tiny logging community of Fort

St. James surrounded by snow-capped mountains and heavily wooded areas. Like many Canadian boys, he played minor hockey and participated in the 2002 Challenge Cup, an international hockey tournament held annually in Vancouver.

Legebokoff's grandfather, Roy Goodwin, who hunted grouse and fished with his grandson, said Cody had a "good upbringing—everything was perfect. We did everything and he was a perfectly normal child. He was no different than you or I when we were younger."

After graduating from a Fort. St. James Secondary School in 2008, Legebokoff took on a job as a mechanic with a Ford dealership and had a steady girlfriend who attended the College of New Caledonia. He lived in an apartment with three close female friends in the nearby town of Prince George.

A friend who knew Legebokoff while in school told the *Vanderhoof Omineca Express* that Legebokoff never showed any signs of violence. "He was very sociable and kind-hearted…didn't hurt others." The friend added, "He went missing for a few weeks before the murder [Loren Donn Leslie], like right before, and he didn't tell anyone where he went, he just disappeared."

He also lived in Lethbridge, Alberta for a short time between June 2008 to August 2009. "Everybody liked him, there wasn't a person that had a bad thing to say about him—nobody," said the grandfather, who last saw Legebokoff a month before his November 2010 arrest when he showed up at a Thanksgiving dinner with a girlfriend. "There's a split personality or something wrong in his head. He needs a doctor to help him."

While awaiting trial at the Prince George Regional Correctional Centre for the alleged murder of Loren Donn Leslie, Legebokoff's troubles were about to get a lot worse.

On October 9, 2010, a decomposed body was found on the edge of a road leading up the mountainside on the edge of L.C. Gunn Park, southeast of the city by RCMP officers with a police dog patrolling the area while following up on an unrelated investigation. The body had been dragged up against a tree line and left, naked from the waist down, with her pants rolled down over her feet. The park is located next to Highway 16, five minutes from downtown Prince George and has dirt roads that extend into a wooded area above the Fraser River.

The remains were identified as Cynthia Frances Maas, a thirty-five-year-old aboriginal woman who police say was involved in prostitution and drugs. She was the mother of a young girl. She was last seen on September 10 in Prince George in the vicinity of Juniper Street and 19 Avenue. Family and friends became concerned when Maas hadn't been heard from over the course of several weeks and reported her missing on September 23. It was not known if Maas was killed in the park or dumped there after she was killed elsewhere. Her cause of death was blunt force trauma to the head and penetrating injuries to the right chest and neck.

Jill Stuchenko, 35, was a mother of four boys and two girls and worked as an escort for several Prince George agencies. She was a talented singer who tried numerous times to walk away from the sex trade life without success. She was reported missing on October 22, 2009. Stuchenko was found dead half-buried in a shallow grave in a gravel pit off Otway Road which backs onto several homes in a newer subdivision near the edge of Moore's Meadow. It was a popular spot for hiking and bush parties on the outskirts of Prince George. Police said she'd likely been dead for seven to ten days. Stuchenko died from massive blunt force trauma to her head. The amount of blood loss was so extreme that the pathologist had trouble obtaining a sample during the autopsy.

Rikki Black, the owner of the Black Orchid escort agency in Prince George, said she knew Stuchenko for over ten years. She stated Stuchenko worked for her agency and took on shifts with other escort agencies and freelanced on the streets as a sex-trade worker. Black described her as a good person who loved her children and had a beautiful voice. Stuchenko allegedly had a drug addiction she couldn't shake.

In the cases of Jill Stuchenko and Cynthia Maas, the RCMP said the crime scenes were examined using the latest in forensic collection and analysis methods. One of the cases was sent to the same forensic specialist in Pennsylvania used in the Loren Donn Leslie case. The forensic expert utilized state of the art computer technology to forensically examine some of the evidence.

Natasha Lynn Montgomery, 23, a mother of two small children was originally from Quesnel, 120 kilometers south of Prince George. She and her long-time boyfriend, who had known each other since she was twelve, had separated over her drug use. According to family and friends, she was an avid baseball player and an accomplished figure skater who'd lost her way over the years. Her last phone call was made to her mother sometime around August 26. Montgomery was reported missing the same day as Cynthia Maas was last seen in the Prince George area.

On October 17, 2011, the RCMP charged Legebokoff with three counts of first-degree murder in the deaths of Jill Stacey Stuchenko, Cynthia Frances Maas, and Natasha Lynn Montgomery. The charges against Legebokoff were the result of a 10-month investigation dubbed *Project E-Prelude*, a joint investigation headed by investigators from the North District Major Crime Unit and the Prince George RCMP Detachment Serious Crime Unit along with support staff and investigators from the E Division Serious

Crime Unit, Behavioral Science Group, the E Division Interview Team, Criminal Analysts and a score of specialized RCMP Forensic Laboratories throughout Canada.

During a news conference in Prince George, police said their investigation was not close to being over as they were searching for witnesses and possibly more victims. It's also believed Legebokoff acted alone.

"He wasn't known to us," said Royal Canadian Mounted Police Inspector Brendan Fitzpatrick, a superintendent in charge of operations for the RCMP's E Division major crime unit. "He had a minor criminal record if anything at all."

The RCMP also said the murders weren't related to the Highway of Tears cases. "We've done that through forensics, and also you just have to look at his [Legebokoff's] age in comparison to the victims," RCMP Insp. Brendan Fitzpatrick said. However, they weren't ruling out the possibility Legebokoff might be linked to other cases.

In the spring of 2012, police renewed public awareness around their efforts to locate Natasha Montgomery. With the change of seasons and warmer weather, they had already conducted searches in high priority areas and were looking to identify additional areas to search which included regions between Prince George, Vanderhoof and

Fort St James.

The RCMP said there was evidence to support the 'no body' murder charge.

◆ ◆ ◆

On March 19, Montgomery's family along with the Sekanni Carrier Nation completed a ceremony at the residence, an apartment, where police believe Natasha was killed. The aboriginal praying and smudging ceremony were carried out in hopes of allowing the Montgomery family to begin to heal.

"While Cody Legebokoff has been charged and will be tried for the death of Natasha, we still need to know where she is in order to give her family the dignity of a proper burial", said Cst. Lesley Smith, North District RCMP Media Relations Officer. "She was a beautiful, loving and caring person. Her family wants to bring her home." To date, her body has not been found.

Securing a murder conviction without a victim's body is typically a rare occurrence, however, Prince George has seen two cases between 2010 and 2011. Denis Florian Ratte was found guilty in December 2011, of killing his wife Wendy Ratte in 1997 even though her body was never found. According to Tad DiBiase, a Washington, D.C.-based prosecutor, there are three ways to prosecute without a body: forensic evidence, confession to friends and family or a confession to police. In the Ratte's case, the accused had confessed to law enforcement. With advances in forensic technology over the past fifty years in DNA, fingerprints, blood and other forms of identification, there has been an increasing number of successful 'no body' prosecutions.

"We proceed with prosecution if the available evidence provides a substantial likelihood of conviction, even if that is based largely on material evidence. Most murder prosecutions do have the presence of a body as part of the evidence, but it is not exclusively the case in B.C. history. Robert Pickton is certainly one case," said B.C. provincial Crown spokesman Neil MacKenzie.

Canada's most infamous conviction of 'no body' murder was that of Robert Pickton. Police found DNA evidence of 26 missing women on his Lower Mainland pig farm, in addition, his confession to police hinted at least 49 killings. The Crown in the Pickton case concentrated on the six victims with the most likely chance of a conviction and in 2007. He was found guilty on all six.

In May 2013, Mark Bridger was convicted of the murder of a five-year-old girl, April Jones from Machynlleth, Wales who disappeared on October 1, 2012. In court documents, Bridger claimed he killed her by accident with his car and had no idea what he had done with her body after a night of heavy drinking. Forensic evidence, in particular bone fragments and blood matching Jones' told a different story and proved that Jones had been murdered at Bridger's cottage and he had disposed of her body. Her remains were never located despite one of the largest missing person searches in UK history. There have also been wrongful convictions that have left the judicial system leery and the need for stringency on the part of the courts when it comes to evidence in 'no body' cases.

The "Dingo baby" case was originally based on circumstantial evidence in which led to a murder conviction in Australia. Azaria Chantel Loren Chamberlain an Australian baby girl was killed by a dingo in August 1980 during a family camping trip. The parents claimed the baby was taken from their tent by a dingo. The child's mother, Lindy Chamberlain was tried for murder and spent over three years in jail. She was released after a piece of Azaria's clothing was discovered next to a dingo lair. In 2012, thirty-three years after the baby's death, the parent's version of the events was officially confirmed by a coroner.

According to the RCMP, Cody Legebokoff allegedly began killings in 2009 when he was 19, a teenage serial killer who had murdered three women and a 15-year-old girl then dumped their bodies in the backwoods during a year-long killing spree.

Elliott Leyton, a professor of forensic anthropology at Memorial University in St. John's, known for his expertise in serial killers, said it was unusual to have serial-killing allegations against someone alleged to have begun killing while a teenager, as the Crown, has suggested. He also went on to say the majority of serial killers are between the ages of 25 and 55 and act in response to social pressures that escalate into adulthood. A killing campaign requires an organizational ability associated with adulthood "to think things through."

Canada's most notorious teen serial killer Peter Woodcock began his rampage at the age of seventeen by murdering three children from Toronto within a four-month span. His first victim, 6-year-old Wayne Mallette was killed at The Canadian National Exhibition (CNE) grounds on Sept. 16, 1956. Three weeks later, Woodcock picked up 9-year-old Gary Morris in Cabbagetown and strangled him. On Jan. 19, 1957. He also killed Carole Voyce, 4, under the Bloor Viaduct. Woodcock was apprehended in 1997. He was found not guilty by reason of insanity.

While incarcerated during the '60s and '70s at Oak Ridge, a psychiatric facility located in Penetanguishene, psychiatrists worked to find ways to cure psychopathic offenders by feeding them drugs including LSD. When therapy and drugs hailed some success, Woodcock was transferred to Brockville Psychiatric Hospital, a medium-security facility. After he changed his name to David Michael Krueger, he contacted Ottawa convicted killer Bruce Hamill who had been released from the psychiatric facility and convinced Hamill that an alien brotherhood might solve his problems if he helped kill another inmate, Dennis Kerr, a man Woodcock claimed he loved and had rejected his sexual advances. Within the first twenty-four hours of his first-day pass in over 34 years, Woodcock with the help of Hamill butchered Kerr using a hatchet and knives. The murder sent shockwaves through the Ontario forensic psychiatry system. Woodcock confessed to the killing and was sent back to Penetanguishene. He died on March 5, 2010, after spending 53 years in custody.

John Martin Crawford was in his late teens when he killed his first victim in Lethbridge, Alta., in 1981. He was convicted and imprisoned. He went on to kill three more women in Saskatoon in 1992. All of Crawford's victims were aboriginal.

Michael Wayne McGray was convicted of six murders and claimed to have killed a total of 16 people in Canada and the U.S. He killed a seventh victim while in prison in 2010. McGray would have been about 20 when he murdered his first victim in 1985.

Sources

Bailey, Ian. "Tens of thousands of text messages linked to accused serial killer."

The Globe and Mail. Sep. 6, 2012. http://www.theglobeandmail.com/news/british-columbia/tens-of-thousands-of-text-messages-linked-to-accused-serial-killer/article557930/.

Bernard, Renee. "Northern BC man accused of serial killings goes on trial." News1130. October 6, 2013. http://ww.news1130.com/2013/10/06/northern-bc-man-accused-of-serial-killings goes-on-trial/

Bourrie, Mark. "The serial killer they couldn't cure dies behind bars." The Star. March 9, 2010. http://www.thestar.com/news/ontario/2010/03/09/the_serial_killer_they_couldnt_cure_dies_behind_bars.html#article

Bulman, Erica. "Alleged serial killer charged in slayings of 4 B.C. Women." The Toronto Sun. October 17, 2011. http://www.torontosun.com/2011/10/17/alleged-serial-killer-charged-in-slayings-of-4-bc-women.

CBC News. "Fraser Lake homicide victim

gets special examination." December 7, 2010. http://www.cbc.ca/news/canada/british-columbia/fraser-lake-homicide-victim-gets-special-examination-1.906931.

CBC News. "Police ID body found in Prince George." October 16, 2010. http://www.cbc.ca/news/canada/british-columbia/police-id-body-found-in-prince-george-1.878473.

Hawkins, Kristal. "A Body in the Snow." Crime Library–Profiling, Interactive. October 4, 2012.
http://www.trutv.com/library/crime/serial_killers/predators/cody-legebokoff/a-body-in-the-snow.html".

Hoekstra, Gordon. "Women will feel safer after man's arrest for four murders: support group." The Vancouver Sun. October 19, 2011. http://www.vancouversun.com/news/Women+will+feel+safer+after+arrest+four+murders+support+group/5568854/story.html.

Hoekstra, Gordon. "Young man charged with murder of three more northern B.C. Women." The Vancouver Sun. October 18, 2011. http://www.vancouversun.com/news/Young+charged+with+murder+three+more+northern+women/5562769/story.html.

Jiwa, Salim. "Prince George: Life and death of Jill Stuchenko." Vancouverite. October 30, 2009. http://www.vancouverite.com/2009/10/30/prince-george-life-and-death-of-jill-stuchenko/.

MacQueen, Ken. "The country boy at the heart of four murder investigations." Macleans. October 24, 2011. http://www2.macleans.ca/2011/10/24/the-country-boy-at-the-heart-of-four-murder-investigations/.

McMahon, Tamsin. "Cody Alan Legebokoff: The country boy accused in the murders of four B.C. Women." The National Post. October 19, 2011. http://news.nationalpost.com/2011/10/18/cody-alan-legebokoff-suspected-serial-killer/.

Neilson, Mark. "Ban imposed on Legebokoff proceedings." The Prince George Citizen. November 10, 2011. http://www.princegeorgecitizen.com/article/20111110/PRINCEGEORGE0101/311099947/0/princegeorge/ban-imposed-on-legebokoff-proceedings#.

Peebles, Frank. "Legebokoff trial a rare case of missing victim." The Prince George Citizen. November 2, 2011. http://www.princegeorgecitizen.com/article/20111102/

PRINCEGEORGE0101/311029993/-1/princegeorge/legebokoff-trial-a-rare-case-of-missing-victim.

Postmedia News. "Alleged B.C. serial killer's trial could take up to a year." The National Post. October 31, 2011. http://news.nationalpost.com/2011/10/31/alleged-b-c-serial-killers-trial-could-take-up-to-a-year/.

The Canadian Press. "Cody Legebokoff, Prince George Man, Faces More Murder Charges." The Huffington Post. December 17, 2011. http://www.huffingtonpost.ca/2011/10/17/cody-legebokoff-prince-george_n_1015589.html.

The Canadian Press. "Trial for alleged serial killer delayed." The Vancouver Sun. August 29, 2013. http://www.vancouversun.com/news/Trial+alleged+serial+killer+delayed/8846672/story.html.

The Canadian Press. "Trial for alleged B.C. serial killer Cody Legebokoff delayed; now set for Oct. 9." August 28, 2013. http://www.avtimes.net/news/world/trial-for-alleged-b-c-serial-killer-cody-legebokoff-delayed-now-set-for-oct-9-1.604903.

The Daily Beast. "A Teen Serial Killer in Canada?" October 23, 2011. http://

www.thedailybeast.com/articles/2011/10/23/
cody-legebokoff-accused-as-canadian-serial-
killer-who-preyed-on-women.html.

Wikipedia. "Murder conviction without a body." http://en.wikipedia.org/wiki/Murder_conviction_without_a_body#Other_modern_cases

Wikipedia. "Death of Azaria Chamberlain." http://en.wikipedia.org/wiki/Azaria_Chamberlain_disappearance

Wintonyk, Darcy. "Body found in gravel pit is missing mother of six." CTV News. October 31, 2009. http://bc.ctvnews.ca/body-found-in-gravel-pit-is-missing-mother-of-six-1.449385#ixzz2hBwEMY6X.

250 News. "Investigators Rely on U.S. Expert in Loren Leslie Murder Case." December 6, 2010. http://www.250news.com/blog/view/18597/1/investigators++rely+on+u.s.++expert++in+loren+leslie+murder+case.

250 News. "The 'Missing Person' Who's Dearly Missed." October 25, 2010. http://www.250news.com/blog/view/18041/1/the+%27missing+person%27+who%27s+dearly+missed.

250 News. "Family Calls for Help in Finding

Closure in Death of Natasha Lyn Montgomery." March 19, 2012. http://www.250news.com/blog/view/23727/1/family++calls+for+help+in++finding+closure+in+death+of+natasha+lyn+montgomery?id=143&st=20.

CBS News. "Cody Legebokoff sentenced to life on 4 counts of 1st-degree murder."

https://www.cbc.ca/news/canada/british-columbia/cody-legebokoff-sentenced-to-life-on-4-counts-of-1st-degree-murder-1.2768118

2013 BCSC 2178 R. v. Legebokoff on www.courts.gov.bc.ca, Retrieved on Mar 10, 2019.

2014 BCSC 368 R. v. Legebokoff on www.courts.gov.bc.ca, Retrieved on Mar 10, 2019.

2014 BCSC 1746 R. v. Legebokoff on www.courts.gov.bc.ca, Retrieved on Mar 10, 2019.

2016 BCCA 386 R. v. Legebokoff on www.courts.gov.bc.ca, Retrieved on Mar 10, 2019.

CHAPTER EIGHT

Joachim Kroll: Man-Eater

Joachim Georg Kroll was born on April 17, 1933 in Hindenburg, a mining town in Upper Silesia (part of Poland). According to conflicting accounts, he was either the youngest of eight children or the sixth child among a total of nine. He was the runt of the family, a bed-wetter, and had suffered from childhood meningitis. He wasn't an intelligent child, his IQ of 76 was considered borderline as being mentally challenged. After his father was taken prisoner by the Soviets in Russia during World War II, and never made it back home, the family packed up their belongings after the fall of the Third Reich and moved to West Germany's North Rhine-Westphalia in 1947. The family's new living quarters were far from ideal or comfortable, as Joachim lived in a cramped two-room flat which he shared with his mother and six sisters (although some sources state four).

In 1943, at the age of ten, Kroll enrolled

in the Hitler Youth program called the Deutsches Jungvolk, an official youth organization in Germany: a paramilitary establishment. On October 10, 1945, the group was outlawed by the Allied Control Council along with other Nazi Party organizations. Barely illiterate and struggling through approximately five years of schooling (some accounts say three), his mother gave up on his education and Joachim was sent to work on a farm to help support the large family. Kroll would later attribute his involvement of slaughtering animals as an influence in his gruesome crimes.

> *"At the age of 14 or 15 years, the accused was present on several occasions when animals were slaughtered on the farms..." (Translated from German)*

As years passed, his sisters moved out of the family home and married. His mother died in early 1955 when Joachim was 22 years old. Free from his mother's iron grip for the first time in his life, he was alone. Whether the loss of his mother was a contributing factor in Kroll's crimes is unknown but eighteen days following her death something triggered deep inside him and he acted on his sexually violent fantasies by commiting his first rape-murder on February 8, killing a Irmgrad Strehl, an attractive 19-year-old runaway from

Niedersachsen.

Over two decades later, he would recount to the police that he was strolling to the local woods in Lüdinghausen when me met up with Irmgrad wearing a green coat and carrying a book bag. He invited her to join him on the walk and she gladly accepted his offer. When he tried to kiss the young woman, she resisted. Enraged by her rejection, Joachim dragged her kicking and screaming into a nearby barn where he strangled and stabbed her in the neck, killing her almost instantly. In a sexual frenzy with her body still warm, he brutally rapes the young woman. After he was done, he slit open her stomach with a folding, long-bladed knife and disemboweled her corpse as if he was slaughtering a pig on a farm. A year passed and Kroll killed again. This time the victim was a 12-year-old girl named, Erika Schuleter whose innocent chance encounter with Kroll on the street in Kirchellen led to her demise. She was found raped and strangled. After the murder, Kroll went on with life as if nothing had happened. He continued to live alone and earned a modest income from his farm employment.

In 1959, he moved to the city of Duisburg and began a job as a lavatory cleaner for Mannesmann. Not even a new job and home could replace his craving for blood and flesh or acting upon his sexual fantasies. On June 16, 24-year-old Klara Frieda Tesmer was walking in the meadow on the bank of the Rhine River near Rheinhausen when

Kroll approached her. The moment she rejected his advances, he hit her in the head then tried to undress her. During the violent attack he strangled and killed her. Afterwards he raped her. Her naked body was discovered the following day by five boys out riding their bicycles. Ten days after killing Tesmer, Kroll strangled 16-year-old Manuela Knodt in the wooded city park of Essen, Bredeney. Following his usual pattern, he sexually assaulted her after she was dead. But this time he also did something different, taking his fantasies of sexual depravity to a new level. He used a long-bladed knife to mutilate and crave pieces of flesh from her buttocks and thighs, the meatiest parts of her body. But what police didn't know was that Kroll had taken the flesh from Knodt to cook and eat. Then before leaving the park, with his sexual urge still not satisfied, he masturbated over the corpse.

> He "did not know, consequently, that his killing by strangling in connection with the conscious observing the agony of his victim would lead to extreme increase his sexual desire and the highest satisfaction, an experience that he only made in later cases." (Translated from German)

Much like the Strehl's murder, police again believed they were dealing with deranged young perverts because of the amount of semen on the victim's faces and pubic area. A mechanic named, Heinrich Ott, was wrongfully arrested for the crime and sentenced to eight years in prison. Innocent and distraught, he served five years before hanging himself in jail. Despite Kroll's low IQ, he was smart enough to take a bus or train to secluded areas to hunt his prey, lowering his risk of getting caught. He also didn't care about the ages (4-61) of his victims as long as they were female which he believed would lower his chances of being nabbed because the authorities were unlikely to link the murders to one killer due. Joachim Kroll would eventually tell the police years later that he had removed flesh from Manuela Knodt's body because he couldn't afford to purchase meat and wanted to know what human flesh tasted like. This would be his first sampling, a taste test, and won't be his last.

Now confident he could get away with murder, in April of 1962, Kroll couldn't control his thrill to kill and began hunting again. On Easter Day, 13-year-old Petra Giese was visiting a fair with a friend when she was lured away to the forest outside the town of Dinslaken-Bruckhausen, north of Duisburg where Kroll strangled with her with her own scarf and then proceeded to rape her. When he was finished, he removed both buttocks as well as the left forearm and hand. Giese's cut up body was discovered in some bushes the following day. Originally the police arrested a minor sex-offender and pedophile by the name of Vinzenz Kuehn for the murder. He was sentenced to 12 years in prison and psychiatric treatment. He was released after 6 years.

On June 3, thirteen-year-old, Monika Tafel, was on her way to school in Walsum when Kroll snatched her and dragged into a rye field. He strangled the teenager, raped her and masturbated over her body. Afterwards, he sliced steaks from her buttocks and the back of her thighs. According to one source, there were signs that the killer might have devoured parts of the girl "on the spot". Her remains were found on June 11 by a police helicopter in the forest outside of the town.

Again, another innocent man was arrested for a crime he didn't perpetrate. Walter Quicker was an ex-Legionnaire and known pedophile. The police were forced to release him due to the lack of physical evidence, but his neighbours continued to prosecute him, and his wife divorced him. Faced with non-stop acquisitions and rumors, on October 5, 1962, Quicker strolled into the dense forest and hung himself from a tree.

On September 3, 12-year-old Barbara Bruder was abducted on her way to the playground near her home in Burscheid-Klien-Hamberg. She was sexually assaulted and strangled. Although, Kroll admitted to killing the little girl fourteen years later too many years had gone by for authorities to visit the crime scene. Her remains were never found.

Then Kroll's usual pattern shifted drastically.

Three years passed and Joachim Kroll's desperately needed to hunt. On August 22, 1965 in lover's lane near a lake in Grossenbaum-Duisburg, Kroll spotted a couple making out in their Volkswagen and he became sexually excited by what he saw.

Twenty-five-year-old Hermann Schmitz was with his girlfriend, Rita (some sources stated her name was Marion). With his victim in sight, he needed to find a way to lure Schmitz from the vehicle. Even though he didn't usually kill males, he came up with a plan. Kroll shoved his knife into one of the tires to flatten it to draw Schmiz out of the car. When the man emerged from the car, Kroll stabbed him in the heart twice and killed him immediately. But he wasn't expecting Rita to immediately jump into the driver's seat, honk the horn repeatedly and trump the gas petal down nearly hitting him before he fled into the forest. Armed with Rita's description of the killer, the police never developed any leads as to who had killed Schmitz. Spooked by nearly getting caught, Kroll laid low for another year.

On September 15, 1966, near Duisburg, twenty-year-old Ursula Rohling was found in some bushes, strangled. She had been dead for almost two days. Her body had been stripped from the waist down and she was provocatively posed. Since her fiancé was with her that night, police treated Adolf Schickel as a suspect even though he had told them the couple had ice cream together and had discussed their upcoming wedding plans before he left Rohling and watched her walk to the park where her remains were discovered. Her fiancé crumbled over the public and police pressure of being falsely accused and threw himself into the Maine River near Wiesbaden.

Joachim Kroll later admitted that he had killed Urusla Rohling, even describing how he had met her in the park, spoke with her, and then shlepped her body into the bushes.

"I saw this woman in the park. She was young, with short hair. I spoke to her and then grabbed her around the neck with my right arm. I dragged her into the bushes and threw her on the ground. I choked her until she stopped moving. Then I took off her pants and her other things and I did it to her. I left her lying there and took the train back to Duisburg. When I got home I was still hot, and I had it with the doll, and did it with my hand a couple of times".

With another young woman murdered and another innocent man accused of a crime he didn't commit, dead, nothing mattered to Kroll other than feeding his hunger. It wasn't long before he was lurking in the area searching for his next victim. And within three months he struck again.

❖ ❖ ❖

On December 5, 1966, five-year-old Ilona Harke was abducted in Essen. Kroll took the little girl on a city train to Wuppertal. They boarded a bus and got off somewhere in an isolated wooded area where he continued for about 500 meters through the thick vegetation to a ditch named 'Feldbach' where he wanted to see "how someone drowned". The small body of Ilona Harke was discovered in the frigid waters of a stream in Wuppertal. She had been raped. Kroll would later recount how he had encountered the child and thought she would be easy to subdue because of her size. He forced her head into the water and held it there until she stopped struggling. Anticipating that she would taste sweet due to her age and size, Kroll experimented. This time he removed flesh from various areas of her body including cutting into one of her shoulders.

About six months later, Kroll tried again after he had temporarily moved to Grafenhausen. On June 22, 1967 between Grafenwald and Grafenhausen, north of Bottrop, he lured 10-year-old Gabriele Puetman into a meadow and showed her pornographic pictures he'd brought along with him. The child was terrified and tried to get away. Kroll began to choke her, but sudden sirens from the mine alerting a shift change scared him. With the area teaming with miners returning home from their shift at the local coal mine, he managed to high tail it out of the area without anyone seeing him believing the child was dead. She wasn't. She was found and taken to a nearby hospital where she remained in a coma for a week. It wasn't until nine years after the arrest of Joachim Kroll when Puetman's parents finally reported the incident to the police.

By the end of the year, Kroll was back working in Duisburg and had an apartment at number 11 Friesenstrasse in the suburb of Laar, a three-room flat with a shared lavatory. After almost getting caught, two years went by before he started hunting again.

By the late 1960s, German authorities were busy conducting a wide-spread search and intense investigation for the killer known as the "Ruhr Hunter". Even with the large police shadow, nothing could stop Kroll's urge to kill.

On July 12, 1969, Kroll took a train trip to from Duisburg to Essen, then a bus to Werden and strolled the banks of the Baldeney Lake. There he met his oldest victim, a 61-year-old pensioner, Maria Hettgen. Kroll later stated that he'd experienced a "tingling" feeling all over his body when he started talking to her. When she didn't wish to carry on a conversation with him, Kroll hit her and dragged her into the bushes where he strangled and raped her. He cut flesh from parts of his body which he would later admit he had consumed as he continued his travels. Hettgen's body was discovered a day later.

On May 21, 1970, Jutta Rahn, a 13-year-old, disembarked from a train in Breitcheid and started walking home through a wooded area between Essener Straße and the Hösel Railway Station. She was found strangled and raped. Like many of Kroll's other victims, Rahn's neighbour and part-time boyfriend, Peter Schay, was arrested for her murder. He spent 15 months in prison before being released due to lack of evidence.

After Kroll murdered, Jutta Rahn, the urge to kill apparently disappeared for almost six years or perhaps he was being cautious after his last kill. In the summer of 1976, he travelled 15 miles north to Dinslaken Vorede on the bank of the River Rhine where he raped and strangled ten-year-old Karin Toepfer. Now a middle-aged man, Kroll lived alone in his flat in Duisburg and became popular with the neighbourhood children. He'd tell them jokes and give them sweets. Known as "Uncle Joachim", he would invite the children into his apartment luring them with dolls and toys. What parents weren't unaware of were the other things hiding in his apartment, the electronic gadgets and inflatable sex dolls. He would use the dolls to fulfil his sexual fantasies, frequently strangling the inflatable rubber while masturbating. At the time, no one gave much notice as to the attention he was giving to the children. With a bulb-shaped face, large ears, and glasses, parents simply believed he was a "harmless old bachelor" so when 4-year-old Marion Ketter vanished while playing at a park on July 3, 1976, suspicion was never cast on Kroll. It wasn't until the next day when the police visited 11 Friesenstrasse that they encountered an agitated man, Oscar Muller, rushing out of the house to get help due to a conversation he had with Kroll. Muller was on the way to use the shared toilet in the apartment block when his neighbour, Joachim Kroll, stopped him.

"You can't use the toilet, it's blocked," said Kroll.
"Blocked? What with?" asked Muller.
"Guts," replied Kroll.

Muller really wasn't sure if Kroll was joking. After all, the man appeared not too smart and completely harmless. But when a plumber along with the authorities investigated the blockage, the toilet contained "bloody liquid and floating flesh" which was later identified by the medical examiner as a heart, kidneys and lungs of a small child. When questioned, Kroll told police he had killed a rabbit to make stew and attempted to flush the internal organs down the toilet.

One of the detectives thought the short and balding man might have been telling the truth since the house smelled like a home-cooked meal. When he was about to taste-test the meal simmering in a pot, Kroll admitted that his recipe included body parts of Marion Ketter. Small chunks of flesh and a hand from the 4-year-old were floating among a mixture of vegetables. Other body parts were discovered wrapped in the refrigerator and freezer. Even the most hardened and seasoned officers were sickened by what they witnessed. Joachim Kroll was immediately arrested.

At first, Kroll admitted to only killing Marion Ketter, but as time passed and the more comfortable, he became behind bars, he began to speak about the murders including murders the police weren't aware had happened. He even offered to take detectives to the locations where he had killed and butchered his victims. Eventually he admitted to 13 murders. He also told the authorities that he only stalked women and girls that would be the "tastiest morsels". He said he had left some of the corpses completely intact because he didn't think their flesh would appeal to his taste buds. Marion Ketter was Joachim Kroll's final victim ending the long search for the cannibalistic lust-murderer and halting a killing spree that spanned a jaw-dropping twenty-one years. He had evaded the authorities due to the erratic pattern of his heinous crimes and that sometimes years went by between the killings while during other years he was manically murdering, cooking and eating his victims. The only thing consistent in each crime was the aggressive sexual act inflicted in most case after death. Even though the grisly murders had some similarities including that the crime area was not large, less than 50 miles in length and width only 20 miles away, police were not able to link any of the cases together. Over time, his fear of getting caught diminished completely.

> *"Later on, I was no longer afraid, if I had killed someone." (Translated from German)*

While in custody, Kroll admitted to what he called a "severe illness of cannibalism". Authorities called him "mentally defective". *Kroll* naively believed he would receive a simple operation that would magically cure him of his homicidal urges, and then he'd be released from prison. Instead he was charged with eight murders and one attempted murder. When asked why he killed children in particular, he made it clear that he never wanted to appeal to older girls because they laughed and made fun of him. During this rambling confession, Kroll told police how he practised strangling blow up dolls while he masturbated giving him the thrill and confidence to move up the ladder to human victims. He also complained about how quality chicken and beef in

Germany had always been too high priced for the working class. This was his excuse as to why he ate parts of his victims.

As the horrific details of necrophilia rape, dismemberment and cannibalism emerged, the pubic demanded that Kroll be executed but capital punishment had been abolished in West Germany in 1949. There were also numerous death threats made against Kroll by bereaved and enraged fathers who had lost their children to the demented killer. On April 8, 1982 after a 151-day trial in Saal 201 of the Duisburg Schwürgericht, Kroll was given nine terms of life-imprisonment and not surprisingly showed any emotion or remorse for his crimes. Over the years, Germany has had numerous serial killers who ate the flesh of their victims. Kroll had been compared to other killers such as, Georg Grossman, known as "The Berlin Butcher" who dismembered, consumed and sold the flesh of up to fifty women, mainly prostitutes and Karl Denke, a church organist who had killed and ate body parts of over thirty of his victims. To many, Kroll will always be known as the *The Ruhr Cannibal, The Ruhr Hunter and the Duisburg Man-Eater* for his sick hunger for the *"sweetest meat"* as well as a sexual sadist, predator and psychopath who never showed any empathy for his crimes. After serving a little more than nine years, Joachim Kroll died of a heart attack at the age of 58 on July 1, 1991 in the prison of Rheinbach, near Bonn.

Sources

Marlowe, John. *Forcible Confinement: Monstrous Crimes of the Modern Age.* Arcturus Publishing, 2014.

Nash, Robert Jay. *The Great Pictorial History of World Crime, Volume 2.* Rowman & Littlefield. 2004.

Ramsland, Katherine. *Bait and Switch: The Cannibal Crimes of Joachim Kroll.* February 10, 2012. http://dingeengoete.blogspot.ca/2012/02/bait-and-switch-cannibal-crimes-of.html

Die morbide Vorstellungs-und Erlebniswelt sadistischer. Serienmörder. *Veröffentlicht in:* Stephan Harbort published in Robertz, F. / Thomas, A. (Hrsg.), Serienmord. Kriminologische und kulturwissenschaftliche Skizzierungen eines ungeheuerlichen Phänomens, 2002. http://www.der-serienmoerder.de/scripts_de/aufsaetze/serienmoerder05.doc

ABOUT THE AUTHOR

Kim Cresswell resides in Ontario, Canada and is the award-winning author of the action-packed WHITNEY STEEL series.

Her romantic thriller, *Reflection* (A Whitney Steel Novel - Book One) has won numerous awards: RomCon®'s 2014 Readers' Crown Finalist (Romantic Suspense), InD'tale Magazine Rone Award Finalist (Suspense/Thriller), UP Authors Fiction Challenge Winner, Silicon Valley's Romance Writers of America (RWA) "Gotcha!" Romantic Suspense Winner, and an Honorable Mention in Calgary's (RWA) The Writer's Voice Contest.

Kim signed a 3-book translation deal with Luzifer Verlag for the first three books in the Whitney Steel series: *Reflection, Retribution,* and *Resurrect.* The popular series will be published in German beginning in 2019.

The Assassin Chronicles TV series, based on Kim's upcoming 4-book paranormal/supernatural thriller series: *Deadly Shadow* (May 2018), Invisible Truth, Assassin's Prophecy, and Vision of Fire was in development with Council Tree Productions.

www.kimcresswell.ca
www.facebook.com/KimCresswellBooks
http://twitter.com/kimcresswell

ALSO BY KIM CRESSWELL

The Whitney Steel Romantic Thriller Series
Reflection (Book One)
Retribution (Book Two)
Resurrect (Book Three)

The Sum of all Tears Series
Icehaven (Book One)
Liberty (Book Two)

The Raina Storm Thriller Series
Dawn of the Storm (Book One)
Dawn of the Enemy(Book Two)

Single Title Novellas
Lethal Journey

True Crime Quickie Short Story Series
Real Life Evil
Murder on Sunset Strip
Garden of Bones
Edge of Madness
Chameleon

Backwoods Murder

Published by Grinning Man Press
Serial Killer Quarterly, "21st Century Psychos"
Serial Killer Quarterly, "Partners in Pain"
Serial Killer Quarterly, "Unsolved in North America"
Serial Killer Quarterly, "Cruel Britannia"
Serial Killer Quarterly, "They Almost Got Away"
Serial Killer Quarterly, "Lostmord: Murder in German"

www.ingramcontent.com/pod-product-compliance
Lightning Source LLC
Chambersburg PA
CBHW060824050426
42453CB00008B/583